Where The Bluebonnets Grow

Where The Bluebonnets Grow

Virginia Pipkin Hurlburt
Billie Pipkin Matthews

EAKIN PRESS ★ Austin, Texas

FIRST EDITION

Published in the United States of America
By Eakin Press, P.O. Box 23069, Austin, Texas 78735

ISBN 0-89015-619-0

Library of Congress Cataloging-in-Publication Data

Hurlburt, Virginia Pipkin, 1929–
    Where the bluebonnets grow.

    Summary: When eleven-year-old Emily Cartwright moves to Texas Territory with her family she experiences snakes, Indians, and Mexican bandits before witnessing the fall of the Alamo and eventually beginning the happy new life they had come to find.
    1. Texas — History — Revolution, 1835–1836 — Juvenile literature.
2. Texas — History — Revolution, 1835–1836. 3. Frontier and pioneer life —
Fiction.   I. Matthews, Billie Pipkin, 1934–.   I. Title.
PZ7.H95659Wh   1987   [Fic]   87-7049
ISBN 0-89015-619-0

To our husbands,

Bob Matthews and Bill Hurlburt,

with much love.

Contents

Introduction

The Cartwrights arrive in the Mexican-ruled frontier territory called Texas during one of the most turbulent periods in Texas history, 1835–36. They settle on the Guadalupe River near Gonzales, joining old friends and meeting new ones who are characters in the authors' previous book, *Clouds Over Texas*. War with Mexico is imminent.

High adventure awaits eleven-year-old Emily Cartwright and her tomboyish girlfriend, Cassie Waggoner, in the untamed territory roamed by Comanches and *banditos*. After being whisked away into captivity by *banditos,* the girls find themselves in the midst of the Mexican army as they march to San Antonio de Bexar. They are present during the fall of the Alamo and hear the Mexican version of the siege. After their escape, they join in the Runaway Scrape with men, women, and children fleeing the Mexican army as it moves across the territory.

1

The Accident

The morning was sunny and bright and the woods were alive with the sound of the mockingbird and the gobble-gobble of the wild turkey. Eleven-year-old Emily Cartwright rocked and jolted on the wagon seat between Mama and Papa. The trail had been so incredibly rough that merely hanging onto her seat demanded her complete concentration. But now they had reached a smoother stretch, allowing her the chance to examine the little wildflower she had picked earlier that morning when they stopped to rest the mules. She turned the wilted, limber stem slowly and tenderly in her hand.

"Mama! Look! These dainty little blooms are shaped like perfect tiny bonnets! Aren't they the deepest, most beautiful blue you ever saw?" she exclaimed, holding the stem up to give her mother a closer look.

"Well, I'll declare! They surely are," said her mother, taking the little flower and studying it with interest. "It must have been a late bloomer. This time of year spring flowers have usually come and gone." She handed it back to Em.

"This was the only one I saw. There wasn't another flower around anywhere that I could see," said Em.

It never once occurred to Em that Papa was paying a smidgen of attention to their woman talk until he grinned down at her and said, "They're no bluer than those two eyes of yours, my dear."

"Well, Mama says I got the color of my eyes from you."

"That may be true, but you got those dark curls from her," replied Papa, "and what a nice combination that is."

Em looked up at her father with adoring eyes and smiled at him. Then, tilting her head to one side, she gazed off into the distance for a moment. Deep in thought, she squinted her blue eyes and pursed her lips. All at once she grabbed her mother's arm excitedly.

"I've got it! I'll call them bluebonnets. That's a good name for them, isn't it, Mama?"

"I'd say it's perfect," her mother replied.

Suddenly one of the wagon wheels struck a big rock, taking Em completely unaware and tossing her a foot into the air. Papa's strong hand reached to keep her from tumbling backwards into the canvas-covered bed of the wagon.

"By jinks! You've got to have wings before you can fly, Em!" he said, tossing his head back in a hearty laugh. He whipped the reins and clucked at the team, urging them onward.

"Settle down, Jake!" he shouted at the old gray mule with the bad disposition.

Anchoring herself tightly to the seat with one hand, Em pushed impatiently at the dark brown, almost black, curl that had worked its way from beneath her bonnet and over her left eye. As if things weren't going bad enough for her, she looked down and spied the little flower. It lay crushed under her foot.

"Oh, now see what those mules have made me do!" she cried, bending to retrieve what was left of the mangled bluebonnet.

"Don't fret, honey. I'm sure, come next spring,

there'll be fields of them for you to pick and enjoy," said Mama, trying to soothe her ruffled feelings.

"I do believe Old Jake and Hannah have deliberately pulled this wagon over every single solitary rock and hole on the trail between here and Missouri. My whole insides feel like they're all in a jumble," complained Em.

"Maybe you won't have to be bumped and bounced around much longer," said Papa with a chuckle. He seemed to be lighthearted.

Em gave him a puzzled look. "Why do you say that, Papa? I don't know what you mean."

"Well, if my calculations are correct, we ought to be reaching our place on the Guadalupe River hours before the sun sets today. Reckon you can manage to hang on that long, little girl?" he asked, winking at her and tweaking the long springy curl that jiggled up and down on her back.

"Today, Papa?"

"That's right," he replied.

"Then we'll be seeing Uncle Wash today! And Cassie! Oh, I'll be seeing Cassie soon too!" she cried, clapping her hands gleefully. She could hardly wait to see her favorite uncle and her best friend, Cassie Waggoner. A smile played across her lips as she thought of that tomboyish friend of hers with the fiery-red mop of hair and freckles to match. She adored her. What kind of mischief had Cassie been up to during the months they were separated? Wonder how she had managed without Em's restraining hand to keep her out of predicaments? She was continually into some kind of escapade.

"Ah, Miriam. What Wash wrote to us about this land is all true. But words just can't describe what we're seeing. It's even more than I ever dreamed," said Papa, bringing Em out of her reverie. His broad shoulders heaved a satisfied sigh. Papa was indeed taken with the land. Em could not remember ever seeing him so joyful. Mama grinned fondly at him.

Em wondered what kind of home Uncle Wash had

3

made ready for them in this new land. She was very eager to find out, but she was even more eager to see Uncle Wash. She idolized her father's younger unmarried brother and had missed him terribly since he left Missouri for Texas territory. He had left several weeks ahead of them to join Green DeWitt's colony and to make legal arrangements for their land. Cassie's folks had loaded their belongings and left Missouri at the same time. Uncle Wash wrote that they had settled on land right up the Guadalupe River from the place he had found for them.

As they burrowed deeper into the territory, Papa's "Texas fever" fairly raged. He said he could now understand how this undeveloped Mexican province was like a giant magnet, drawing people from all over the South. Its vast forests teemed with wildlife, and its smiling prairies begged for the lifting and turning of the plow. They had forded clear streams brimming with fish and had rumbled across fresh green riverbottoms thick with trees trickling with honey. Uncle Wash had written of the great herds of wild horses and buffalo he and Uncle Karl had seen roaming the prairies — there just for the taking.

The sheer abundance of everything seemed to overwhelm Papa. His excitement rose to a fever pitch as they drew nearer to their destination. Em moved close to him and hugged his arm. She felt good because he seemed so happy.

Suddenly a sharp *crack* sounded. The wagon lurched forward and the mules went berserk. Papa leaped from the wagon, still grasping the reins. Old Jake reared and then bolted to the left, causing the wheels to cut sharply and scrape hard against the side of the wagon. Em gripped the seat tightly as the right side of the wagon lifted high into the air and teetered on two wheels. Squeezing her eyes shut, she waited for it to topple on its side, but the wheels finally dropped heavily to the ground. It seemed as if her teeth were jarred right out of her head. Papa dug his heels into the dirt and pulled back on the reins with all his might.

"Whoa, mules! Whoa!" he roared.

Hannah began to settle down some, but Old Jake continued to snort and stomp and toss his head. In a calm voice, Papa talked to the agitated animals until they finally quieted and stood still.

His muscular shoulders hunched impatiently and he shook his head as he surveyed the damage. Turning to Mama and Em, he said, "The trace broke where it fastens to the singletree on Jake's side of the wagon. That's what forces the team to work together pulling the wagon. We can't go another foot until I get it fixed. Old Jake's too stubborn to cooperate and pull his fair share of the load without it. Miriam, I'd rather you and Em were out of the wagon while I'm working. That ornery Jake might pull another shenanigan and turn the wagon over. He's awfully hard to control when he gets excited."

"Well, I've been considering walking the rest of the way, anyway," said Em, rubbing her stomach for a second before she jumped to the ground.

Mama pulled a quilt from the wooden box in the wagon and spread it on the ground in the cool shade of a sleepy old elm. Em promptly flopped down on it, stretched out, and closed her eyes. She savored every single moment away from the churning and jolting of the wagon. Just as she had wriggled herself into a comfortable position for a nice rest, she heard a droning sound. Her eyes popped open and instantly focused on a large pear-shaped blob swinging from a limb right above their heads. It was alive with nervous activity. Springing to her feet, she dashed away from the tree.

"Mama! Run! Hornets!" she cried, pointing to the busy nest. Mama snatched up the quilt and was out from under the tree in a flash. Em couldn't help but giggle. She had no idea her mother was capable of such speed.

From a distance they warily watched the large black insects with yellow bands encircling their bodies. They buzzed in, out, and around the nest that hung unsteadily from the low-hanging branch.

"They're really angry," said Mama.

"Now I know where that old saying 'mad as a hornet' comes from. Ugh! The stingers on those things must be at *least* an inch long," said Em, shuddering.

"Well, not quite," Mama replied with a grin. "That's exaggerating it a bit. I'm sure it might feel like it was an inch long if one stung you, though. By the way, they may be menacing insects, but they're also useful. Their young eat flies, caterpillars, and other insects harmful to man. And — this little tidbit will probably surprise you — did you know they were the very first paper makers?"

"They were?" asked Em, lifting her eyebrows as she gazed at the hornets.

"They surely were. When they build a nest, they chew old wood and tough plant fibers to a pulp, mixing much of their saliva with it. Then they form it into felt-like masses for their nests. It's real paper. They say the Chinese invented paper after watching them build their nests."

"They may be smart and they may be useful, but Papa says I don't ever want one to sting me. He said when he was a boy he had a hunting dog that got stung by a hornet, and the hair around the place where the stinger went in turned as white as snow in a few days. They must be able to do some real damage with those stingers," said Em, ducking out of the path of one that zoomed past her toward the wagon.

She watched it zip around and around in circles then dart here and there. She held her breath when it suddenly landed on the burly rump of Old Jake, driving its venomous stinger deep into the old gray mule's flesh. With a mighty surge, Jake brought his hind legs up in a powerful swift kick. She heard the thud when they hit Papa. He reeled backwards and crumpled in a heap on the ground.

Mama dived for the reins and struggled to control

6

the frightened mules while Em ran to her father and fell to her knees beside him. Panic gripped her. Papa's eyes were closed, and he was as pale and lifeless as death itself.

"Papa! Papa!" she screamed, stroking his face with her trembling hands. Was he breathing? She could not see the rise and fall of his chest. "Hurry, Mama!" she cried before she realized that her mother was already bending over him, fumbling nervously to find a pulse. Out of her agonized eyes suddenly sparked a ray of hope.

"Oh, he's alive! He's alive, Em!" Grateful tears spilled down her cheeks. "Run to the wagon and get some water out of the keg. And get a cloth! Hurry!"

Em never knew how she summoned the strength to pour from the heavy keg, but in a twinkling it was done and she was back by her father's side. They worked in a frenzy, applying one cool cloth after another to his forehead and neck. After what seemed like forever to Em, his eyes fluttered open. The feeble groan that escaped his lips was like heavenly music to her ears.

"You're going to be all right, Papa. You'll be all right," said Em in a trembling voice, looking heavenward and praying silently for the assurance she did not actually feel at that moment.

Papa's lips moved as though he were attempting to speak, but no sound came. Then his eyes closed again. He floated in and out of consciousness. *Oh, Papa, please! Please don't die!* she prayed silently. What great relief she felt when he finally looked up at her with some kind of recognition.

"Zeb, don't try to talk, and don't you worry about a thing. Somehow we'll get help for you. Everything's going to be fine — just fine." Mama's serene voice seemed to soothe him.

"I'll go try to find — " Em's words died in her throat when Mama suddenly clutched her arm. Her eyes grew wide with alarm when she saw the look on her mother's face. Then she heard it too. Something was moving through the woods toward them! Was it a wild animal? A Comanche? A cold chill ran up and down her spine. Like a bolt out of the blue, it flashed into her mind that Papa could not protect them now. What were they to do? She had to think of something fast!

"Mama, I'll get Papa's gun," she whispered hoarsely, making a dash for the wagon.

Just as she laid the weapon in Mama's hands, two figures emerged from the stand of trees — two young boys who appeared to be not much older than Em. They led their horses, and behind them trailed two hunting dogs. Surprise registered on their faces when they discovered they were not alone in those woods. Slowly and cautiously they moved forward. Em's eyes fixed upon them.

"Hello," timidly spoke the one with reddish-blonde hair. The boys stopped a few paces away and gawked curiously at Papa lying on the ground with his head in Mama's lap. "I'm Matt Kincaid and he is Memo Hernandez. Has something bad happened?" he asked.

Em studied the brown-skinned, raven-haired boy beside him. He looked to be of a people entirely unfamiliar to her.

"We're the Cartwrights and my husband has just been injured by that gray mule. We need help desperately — and quickly!" cried Mama.

Matt hurried over to get a closer look at Papa. His sky-blue eyes filled with sympathy. "We'll help you, Mrs. Cartwright. We live just across the woods not far from here. Memo will ride to get my father while I stay here with you. Don't worry. They can get here in only a short while. Papa will know what to do."

The words were hardly out of his mouth before Memo vaulted into his saddle and streaked away through the woods. Em breathed a grateful sigh.

She felt ever so much better with Matt there. The tenseness that knotted every muscle in her small body

Two figures emerged from the stand of trees.

seemed slowly to give way to an unexplainable calmness. She had a deep-down feeling inside that somehow Papa would recover from his injury. He just had to! She yearned to see that gleam of eager anticipation in those blue eyes again. Someday she would. She would not allow herself to believe anything else.

2

Matt Takes Charge

Em was thoroughly impressed with Matt's resourcefulness. He scurried around with an air of confidence, totally in command of the situation. In no time at all he had constructed a tent from dead limbs he dragged from the woods. Over them he draped the quilt Mama had tossed to the ground when the turmoil began. Papa now lay under its protective shade.

How brave he was! Without so much as a moment's hesitation, he swaggered right on up behind Old Jake like he was accustomed to mending broken traces behind an ornery old mule every day of the week. Em opened her mouth to warn him, but before she could manage to utter a sound Old Jake flung his head in the air and backed his ears so flat they looked pasted to his skull. Matt, she discovered, was not only brave, but he was fast too. She had *never* seen anyone move with such lightning speed. If his long legs had not tangled together, she felt quite certain that his giant leap into the air would have easily carried him ten feet from the wagon. As it was, he landed a short but safe distance from the skittish animal.

Em rushed to the side of her glittering hero. "Are you hurt?" she asked anxiously.

"N-a-a-a-w," he drawled, slowly picking himself up out of the dirt. The flush that started at the base of his throat spread upward and made his face so red it almost glowed. "I wanted to give him plenty of kickin' room." He leaned over and looked down at his legs as if he expected to discover some kind of unnatural change in them. "I can't figure out why they're playin' tricks on me lately — always gettin' in my way. I reckon they're just growin' too fast for the rest of my body," he added as some sort of explanation for his clumsiness.

"Maybe I can be of help," said Em. "While you work on the trace, I'll try to keep Old Jake calm the way Papa does."

She moved to stand by the mule's head. As she began to speak gently into Old Jake's ear, Matt inched cautiously toward the trace until he finally held it in his trembling fingers. With one eye on the trace and the other on Old Jake's hind legs, he worked feverishly. In only a few short minutes, crystal beads of sweat glistened on his forehead and his shirt looked like water could be wrung from it.

Em puzzled over the matter for a moment. She had seen a good case of nervousness cause a person to perspire a lot. But Matt was so brave! Surely in this case there must be another good reason. But hard as she tried, she could not think of one.

Finally he straightened slowly, eyeing Old Jake all the while, and eased away from the wagon. "That ought to do it," he said, breathing a ragged sigh. As he surveyed his handiwork from a safe distance, a self-satisfied grin spread across his face from ear to ear. "Yep, I figure no farther than you have to go from here, it ought to hold just fine. You *are* the family from Missouri Mr. Cartwright has been expecting, aren't you?"

"Yes! Oh, yes!" exclaimed Em with surprise and delight. "Do you know my Uncle Wash?"

"I should say I do! He's talked so much about you, I felt like I knew you before we ever met. He'll be happy you've finally arrived. I'll tell you one thing for sure, Mr.

Wash has the finest collection of arrowheads anybody could ever want. I'd give my eyeteeth to have a collection like that. He's so proud of those arrowheads. He carries them around in a nice leather pouch everywhere he goes. Once in a while Memo and I are lucky enough to get to look at them. We have a collection of our own, but it's nothing like the one Mr. Wash has."

Suddenly Em stiffened. "Shh!" she said, placing a finger across her lips.

Out of the distance came the sound of pounding hooves moving in their direction. Em began to edge her way toward her mother.

Matt tilted his head to one side and listened. "Aw, you can relax. It's only Memo and Pa," he said confidently.

"How can you know that for sure?" asked Em, still doubting.

"I can just tell," he replied with a carefree shrug.

Only seconds passed before the riders emerged from the woods. Sure enough, Memo rode toward them waving his *sombrero* as they approached. There was no mistaking the person riding next to him. Matt was only a smaller version of the brawny man with a shock of reddish-blond hair — except, of course, for the handlebar mustache that curled up over each cheek.

"Pa, they're Mr. Wash's kin," called Matt excitedly. "They're Mr. and Mrs. Cartwright and Em."

"I'm mighty pleased to meet you. I'm Jonathan Kincaid. Memo has already told me about the accident. I took it upon myself to send our neighbor, Anson Johnson, into Gonzales to fetch the doctor. I hope I did the right thing."

"Oh, yes! I'm very thankful that you did. I'm afraid Zeb's injury may be very serious," said Mama.

"Memo said he thought it might be pretty bad, but he didn't know how it happened."

"The trace broke and Zeb was trying to fix it when Old Jake kicked him in the stomach," replied Mama.

"It should only take a few minutes to fix it, and then we'll get you on over to your place. It's just a short distance through the woods," he said.

Matt tugged at his father's sleeve. "It's done," he announced proudly.

"What's done?" asked Mr. Kincaid.

"The trace, Pa. It's fixed. Wasn't anything to it," he boasted.

"Well, I do say!" Mr. Kincaid exclaimed, walking over to the wagon to inspect the repair job. Old Jake launched into another fit of quivering and stomping. Mr. Kincaid hastily gave him wide berth. "Son, I would have been very concerned, to put it mildly, had I known you were working so close to this cantankerous mule," he said.

"I was awful careful. I really wasn't *that* scared of him," said Matt, giving Em a sly, sheepish grin.

"You did a mighty fine job of fixing it. Couldn't have done better myself. But, son, that was a dangerous thing you did."

"I tell you what, Pa. Just so you won't worry about me, I *promise* you I won't do *that* again for a very l-o-n-g time — maybe never." He mumbled the last two words under his breath and grinned like a 'possum.

"Well, I certainly am relieved to hear that. It did save us some time. Let's get the wagon ready so we can take them on over to the cabin," he said.

In only a few short minutes, they managed to shuffle things around in the wagon until there was space in the bed of the wagon for Papa and Mama. Very qently they lifted Papa and laid him on the soft stack of quilts Mama had spread in the wagon bed. She climbed in and sat beside him.

"Now — that's that," said Mr. Kincaid. Then he scratched his head thoughtfully. Turning to Em, he asked, "Can you ride a horse?"

"Yessir," she replied meekly.

"Then you ride my horse and visit with the boys while I drive this team," he said, handing her the reins and climbing onto the wagon seat before she had time to explain.

3

Toward Home

It was not an entirely new experience for her. Uncle Wash had allowed her to ride his gentle old horse back in Missouri a few times. Nevertheless, Em felt very inadequate, especially having to ride beside these two expert horsemen.

Climbing awkwardly into the saddle, she sat uneasily for a moment and breathed a heavy sigh. Oh well, there was no getting out of it gracefully now. She clucked at the horse and hoped as they began to move that the boys would not tease her unmercifully. Perhaps by watching them and doing exactly as they did, she could learn quickly and they would never know the difference. As inconspicuously as possible, she cut her eyes around to watch their every move. Her spirits began to rise immediately. To her relief, she found that Matt jiggled and bobbed up and down in the saddle as much as she did. Memo was the one to watch. How *perfectly* he sat in the saddle and handled his mount!

"Memo! Where did you learn to ride like that?" she asked, awed by his skill.

"His father taught him," Matt answered quickly for

15

him. "He was one of the finest horsemen in all of Mexico. Someday I'll ride as well as Memo."

"Matt is learning more and getting better each day. You should see how accurately he shoots a gun. He is teaching me to be a fine marksman like he is," said Memo. Em noticed how modest and polite he was.

"Yep, we teach each other," said Matt. "He's teaching me to ride and I'm teaching him to shoot. That's a pretty good trade, don't you think?"

Poor Matt. They did not have a chance to warn him. He was so busy talking, he did not see the low-hanging limb until it was within inches of his face. With a sharp, quick gasp, he dropped the reins like they were hot and grabbed the limb with both hands to keep from being raked from the saddle. The horse walked right out from under him, leaving him dangling from the branch with a look of panic on his face. When they saw Matt's predicament, Em and Memo howled with laughter until tears coursed down their cheeks.

"Whoa!" Mr. Kincaid commanded the mules.

The wagon creaked to a stop and he jumped to the ground. For an instant he looked startled when he saw Matt. Then he shook his head in bewilderment.

"Matt, what on earth are you doing hanging from that tree?"

"Nothin', Pa," he drawled, looking mortified as he dropped to the ground and climbed back into his saddle. Mr. Kincaid must have figured out what happened. He gave Matt a wry grin, shook his head, and climbed back onto the wagon.

For several minutes they rode in silence. Matt was too embarrassed to utter a word and Em and Memo were about to choke to death on stifled laughter. Finally, Em rode in close to the wagon to see how Papa was faring. He seemed to be tolerating the ride well enough on the smooth stretch of ground. When she saw how pale he looked, she felt guilty for having laughed so loudly while he was sick. She hoped they had not disturbed him. Mama's reassuring smile made her feel much better. Em slowed the horse and rejoined the boys.

Matt bobbed up and down in the saddle, his lips sealed and his head down. Em decided the ridiculous silence had lasted long enough.

"You must know the Waggoners since their place is right next to ours," she said, directing her statement to both boys.

"Sure do," said Matt, slowly cutting his eyes around at Memo.

"As you probably already know, they were our neighbors in Missouri. Then you know Cassie!" she blurted.

If Em was expecting to force a few words from Matt, she got more than she bargained for. The name Cassie seemed to spark something in Matt. He looked at Memo, and Memo looked at him. Then he burst into a torrent of words, hardly stopping long enough to gulp air into his lungs.

"Geeminy! Do we ever know that carrot top! She's not scared of anything — I mean *anything*! Memo and I steer clear of that girl every chance we get. I guess you'd *call* her a girl, but she *acts* more like a boy. Goes around wearin' buckskins like these I have on. And she's *always* got that slingshot of hers dangling from her waist — except, of course, when she's got it whizzin' above her head. When that happens, you'd best take cover, and *fast,* 'cause there's no way of knowin' what she's liable to hit, especially when she's mad.

"She's got the awfullest temper you ever saw and gets riled at the drop of a hat. She'd lots rather carry a gun like Memo and I do, but Mr. Karl won't allow it — thank goodness." Matt stopped for a moment, thinking.

"And *another* thing! She thinks she's got powers — you know, like magic. You see this wart on my thumb?" he asked, thrusting his hand toward Em. "She told me she could make it go away by *spittin'* on it. Can you be-

17

lieve that? Well, she'll never get to prove that one to me 'cause there's no *way* I'm goin' to let her spit on *my* wart.

"She kinda reminds me of that old outcast Comanche who hangs around Mr. Charlie Cole's store sometimes in Gonzales. Claims he can cure people of their ailments. You might keep him in mind if your father doesn't get better soon. I don't know whether he uses some kind of hocus-pocus or whether he's got remedies, but whatever it is, it worked on my dog Old Blue for sure. Cured him slicker'n a whistle that time he got zapped on the side of his head by a big diamondback rattlesnake.

"But gettin' back to Cassie — I just don't *know* about that girl. Poor ol' Memo doesn't either. When we're around her, Memo just stands back and gawks with his mouth wide open. But *I'm* the one she's always pickin' on. That girl should've been a boy. There's no question about it," he said, shaking his head from side to side.

That was Cassie, all right. She apparently had not changed a whit since she left Missouri. Em smiled to herself.

She was very careful to notice that during Matt's speech, Memo continually nodded his head up and down. He obviously agreed fully with every word Matt said.

Feeling a little mischievous, Em decided to get back at them for Cassie. "She's my best friend," she said as casually as she could.

For an instant there was dead silence. Then she heard them gasp as they spun around in their saddles to stare at her in disbelief.

"She's *what?*" they chorused.

"She's my very best friend in the whole world," Em said lightly, relishing every second of their squirming discomfort. She put her hand over her mouth to hide the amused smile that threatened to explode into hearty laughter.

Awkward silence prevailed for several seconds until finally Matt found his tongue and stammered, "Oh, uh — well, uh — I-I guess she's all right — just different from any girl we ever knew. Yeah — she's okay — isn't she, Memo?"

"*Sí!* Oh, yes! She's okay," he replied almost too quickly. He gave Matt an agitated frown as if to say he much preferred being left out of that conversation.

"I'd still be willin' to betcha she could take on the whole Mexican army single-handed and come out the winner," Matt mumbled.

"The whole Mexican army! What on earth are you talking about?" asked Em. Matt seemed to have a real knack for talking in riddles.

"Aw, I was just joshin'. But for sure, I'd rather have her on our side if we have to fight the Mexicans. From all the talk around the settlement, it looks more and more like we may have to do just that. The settlers are having dissension with the Mexican government. I'm sure you know what dissension means," he said importantly.

"Well, no. I don't believe I've ever heard the word," she replied sharply, feeling somewhat miffed at Matt for showing off with his big word.

"Don't feel bad, Em. Matt wouldn't know what it means either if it weren't for Mama Sarah," said Memo, quickly coming to her rescue. "Mama Sarah is one fine teacher, but my brother does not care so much for her lessons. He much prefers to spend time hunting and fishing."

"Your brother?" asked Em, eyeing them curiously.

"Yes. Memo is my brother," Matt spoke up quickly.

"*Sí,*" said Memo simply. Then with a knowing smile spread across his face, he removed his *sombrero* and fondly swatted Matt on the arm with it. "But we must explain to Em, my brother."

"Well, you see, Memo lived across the Guadalupe from us on his ranch. A few months ago a cholera epidemic swept the country and he lost his whole family. Now he lives with us, and my mother and father say he is their boy just like I am. That makes us brothers, doesn't it?"

19

A sadness crept into his voice as he went on. "One day Memo's grandfather who still lives in the southern part of Mexico will come for him. Mama says he probably won't come while we're having so much dissension with the Mexican government. That gets us back to that word. I'd much rather talk about that, anyway. Dissension means disagreement, like we're having with the Mexican government. The government insists that we be Roman Catholics whether we want to be or not. They won't allow us to trade with the United States. Instead, they make us pay higher prices for goods brought in from Mexico. Besides that, they don't trust us. They think we came here to take Texas for the United States."

"Ay-yi-yi! My brother is a much better student than he would lead you to believe. You see? I told you Mama Sarah is one fine teacher," said Memo, tossing his head back in hearty laughter. "Wait until I tell her about this!"

"Aw, come on, Memo," said Matt, turning crimson. "Who could help but learn some of that stuff she tries to pound into our heads? After all, she keeps us prisoner with the books for at *least* a whole hour every day."

Em pondered about that for a moment. She wondered what Matt would do if he had to spend a whole *day* in school like she did in Missouri. Probably perish, she concluded.

Suddenly Matt stood in his stirrups and pointed up ahead of them. "There's your cabin, Em — over there in those trees."

Her heart leaped when she saw it. The log cabin that nestled under the huge liveoaks and elms was crude, but it was beautiful to her after endless days on the long, lonely trail. The cabin would offer protection from the many wild animals that roamed the forest, from Comanches who were always a threat, and from sudden storms that rolled in with little or no warning.

As they approached the cabin, a tall, lean, but powerful figure strode into the front yard. He began to wave his arms excitedly in recognition.

Uncle Wash! He made quite a picture standing there — a real frontiersman clad in buckskins, knee-high boots, and a broad-brimmed hat pulled down over his curly blond hair.

Em nudged the horse with her heel and sped past the wagon to meet him. With a radiant smile on his face, he scooped her from the saddle with his sun-browned hands and gave her a hug that almost squeezed every ounce of breath from her lungs. When he stood her on the ground beside him, he turned his eyes back to the wagon rumbling across the clearing with Mr. Kincaid driving the team. A perplexed look clouded his face.

"Where are your mama and papa?" he asked.

"They're inside the wagon. Papa's hurt. Old Jake kicked him," she said.

"Zeb? Zeb's hurt?" Startled, he took off in a panic toward the wagon.

4

Snake!

Papa was finally settled on the bed in one room of the double-log cabin. Until now there had been no time for Em to pay any attention to her new home. Nothing was left to do now but wait for the arrival of the doctor, so she stepped out into the dog-trot that separated the two rooms of the cabin. She discovered the other room was the kitchen.

No wonder Uncle Wash had become so lean and muscular! In his letters he had written that the neighbors along the river had spent long hours helping him with the building. They helped chop down the trees, strip the logs, and then use a foot adze to scrape them into a four-sided shape. Since their cabin had two rooms, he said it took more than the usual one day for the "house raising."

Each room had one heavy door and a window twelve inches square. He had covered the windows with hide curtains and on the outside had added thick wooden shutters for protection against unfriendly visitors and bad weather. Sturdy bars were built to slide across the doors to hold them shut. Uncle Wash decided against a sod roof since it was not waterproof and cattle might come to feed on it. Instead, he made a roof by splitting oak logs into two and one-half foot lengths, fastening them like shingles to purlins. Papa had explained to Em that a purlin was a part of the roof that lay horizontally to support the rafters. The purlins were then fastened to the end framework of the cabin with pegs. At first the floors were only hard-packed earth, but Uncle Wash had covered them with puncheon, split logs laid with the flat side up.

From the looks of things, Em figured Uncle Wash must have worked day and night. In the middle of the kitchen stood a long wooden table made of several split-log slabs. On either side of it were benches made of smaller slabs. Just wait until Mama saw that cast-iron cookstove standing in one corner of the room! She would be so proud of it. Back in Missouri she had cooked in kettles that hung in the fireplace.

Above the doorway Uncle Wash had hung deer antlers to use as a rack for his gun, bullet pouch, and powder horn. Another pouch hung there too. Em guessed that was the one that contained the collection of arrowheads Matt had mentioned. Spaced here and there were wooden pegs stuck into the logs for hanging clothing and other articles. Uncle Wash must have whittled those in late evenings while he rested after a hard day in the woods and fields.

Near the door were some long pegs stuck into the logs in a vertical row, instead of being irregularly spaced. That was curious, she thought. It appeared to be a ladder reaching up to what she supposed was a loft. Curiosity got the best of her, and up the ladder she climbed.

She could not believe her eyes. There in the loft was a smaller version of Papa's bed. A short pole stuck into the wall formed the outside rail of the bedstead with a notched log holding up the free end. Crosspoles laid from the pole to the side wall held the mattress. The mattress was stuffed with leaves, just like Papa's. Her very own room! She *knew* it must be because Uncle Wash's bed was in the dog-trot.

She scurried down the ladder and sailed past Uncle Wash and Mr. Kincaid, who were sitting in the straight-backed cowhide chairs on the front porch. On second thought, she wheeled around and ran back to give Uncle Wash a grateful hug.

"Say! I liked that, but what was it all about?" he asked, chuckling.

"My room, Uncle Wash! My room!" she exclaimed. Leaping off the porch, she headed for the barn where Matt and Memo were feeding Old Jake and Hannah. Behind the cabin, frail chicken coops dotted the backyard. Em heard the peep of baby chicks and saw them crowding one of the coops. She stopped, stooped over, and gently picked up one of the fluffy little balls of down and stroked it while the old mother hen clucked nervously. Carefully she placed it on the ground beside its mother and skipped on toward the barn.

Before reaching the smokehouse, Em could already smell the smoldering wood used to cure the meat. She opened the door and looked inside. Great slabs of meat hung from pothooks in the ceiling. As she walked past the tool shed, in one corner she saw a nest brimming with eggs. She made a mental note to stop on the way back to the cabin and get them.

From the barn lot came the sound of boyish giggles. Em hurried on to find the source of entertainment. To her surprise, it was Old Jake.

"Come over here, Em. You've just *got* to see this to believe it," said Matt between chuckles. "Old Jake is strange in more ways than one. Watch what he does with this ear of corn," he said, holding it out to the old mule.

Old Jake took the ear of corn between his teeth and worked it around with his tongue, removing the kernels row by row until the cob was clean. Then he rolled the cob around in his mouth until it was lengthwise so he could bite it in half with his teeth. *Crunch! Crunch!* He ate the whole thing while Matt and Memo bent double with laughter.

"I've never seen anything like it. That mule's a neater eater than my brother Matt," Memo teased.

"Now, aren't you the poet!" said Matt, turning his back to Old Jake to pummel the air as if he were jabbing at Memo.

"Watch out!" cried Em, making a beeline for the log fence.

Matt spun around in time to see Old Jake baring his teeth to nip at the seat of his pants. Matt jumped a foot into the air and sailed across the lot, then scrambled over the fence where his friends already waited.

Em giggled hysterically. "He b-bites, t-too," she stammered, wiping at the tears that ran down her cheeks.

"Can you believe that!" exclaimed Matt, glaring at Old Jake. "That's what I'd call mighty ungrateful."

"H-he w-was asking y-you for another ear of c-corn." Em held her sides and bent over in another fit of laughter while Memo collapsed to his knees and hee-hawed. Matt grinned in spite of himself.

As they walked toward the cabin, Matt continued to mumble about that ungrateful old mule. Em could already see that he was the type to get into predicaments without even trying.

Before they reached the tool shed, Em heard a disturbance within. That reminded her. She motioned for Matt and Memo to stop. "Wait for me. I saw something in here I want to take to Mama."

Gathering the corners of her apron, she made a nice basket for the eggs. Two fat old hens with ruffled feathers were perched on the handle of the plow, squawking excitedly as she swept past them.

"Now, hush," she scolded. "I don't intend to bother you at all. I just want the eggs in that nest. You don't need to make such a fuss."

Just as she stooped to get the eggs, she felt something cold and wriggly tighten around her ankles. Her face turned white with terror and she stood frozen like a stone statue. Then her gaze dropped to her feet. A quick, sharp gasp escaped her lips.

"*E-e-e-e-e!*" she screamed, dancing wildly to pull herself from the clinging coil. She did not realize she had broken free until she saw Matt aim the pitchfork and pin the long, black, thick reptile to the ground as it attempted to slither away through an opening between the wall and the ground. Memo chopped at it with a hoe.

Overcome with horror, Em crumpled to the ground. The next thing she knew Uncle Wash was beside her hugging her close while Mr. Kincaid rushed to help Matt and Memo.

"Uncle W-Wash! Th-that aw-awful thing wrapped around m-my ankles," she stammered, shivering uncontrollably. When Matt raised the headless, wriggling body on the tines of the pitchfork, Em gazed in horror for a second and then scooted across the ground away from it.

"Is it still alive?" she cried, unable to tear her eyes away.

Mr. Kincaid took the pitchfork from Matt and quickly disappeared around the corner of the tool shed. Em was relieved to have it removed from her sight.

"Snakes wriggle like that after they're dead. You don't have to be afraid anymore. The old story goes that even without a head, a snake will wriggle until the sun goes down. I don't know whether that's true or not 'cause I never watched one long enough to find out," said Matt.

They heard Mama calling from the cabin door. "She's all right, Miriam," Uncle Wash hollered. "It was only a chicken snake."

"*Only* a chicken snake! It was enough to scare a body to death!" exclaimed Em.

Uncle Wash pulled her up to stand on her wobbly legs and helped her walk to the front porch of the cabin. She dropped weakly to the steps as Mama came rushing out of the kitchen.

"Are you all right, Em?" she asked worriedly.

"I guess so, Mama. There's a whole nest of eggs in

the tool shed I was planning to bring to you, but I think Uncle Wash will have to get them or else just let the snakes have them. I'm not sure I'll *ever* go back into that tool shed again." Mama laid a comforting arm across her shoulder. Then suddenly remembering, Em looked toward the room where her father lay in bed. "How is he, Mama?" she asked.

"He seems to be resting right now, but I'll surely be glad when the doctor gets here."

Mama was afraid. Em could feel her fear. She reached to clasp her mother's hand. "Papa's going to be all right. I know he will," she said.

5

The Reluctant Journey

While they waited for Uncle Anson and the doctor, Em received a lesson on snakes. Though it was certainly not her favorite subject, she decided it would be smart for her to listen, especially after that episode in the tool shed.

"Matt found out as soon as he reached Texas territory that you must watch every step you take out here," said Memo.

"Yeah," said Matt, turning his boot to show Em the scars. "These fang marks were put there by the biggest diamondback rattlesnake you ever saw. If it hadn't been for the tough leather in these boots, I would've been a goner."

"Rattlesnakes usually give a warning before they strike, but copperheads don't," said Memo. "You're very lucky this time. Chicken snakes aren't poisonous. They'll just scare you within an inch of your life."

"There's a way to recognize the poisonous ones without too much trouble," Matt offered. "In this part of the country all poisonous snakes are pit vipers — except for the coral snake. A pit viper has a triangular-shaped

28

head. There's a deep hollow, or pit, in front of each eye and below it, on the side of the head. Rattlesnakes, copperheads, and water moccasins are pit vipers.

"The coral snake is very poisonous too, but its head is rounded, not triangular. It has bright bands of red, yellow, and black around its body. The snout is usually black, and the red and yellow bands are next to each other. Like the old saying goes, 'Red on yellow, kill a fellow.' Some people mistake the harmless kingsnake for a coral snake. They do look very much alike, except that the kingsnake has a red snout and the red and yellow bands are not next to each other," Matt explained with authority.

"Ah-ha! Here we go again! Mama Sarah did her job well. My brother has learned another good lesson, I see," said Memo, clapping Matt on the back teasingly.

"Aw, that subject just happened to be interesting for a change. Better than readin' or writin' or 'rithmetic for sure," said Matt defensively.

"I'm awfully proud of you for paying attention to your mama during that particular lesson, Matt. It could save your life, you know," said Mr. Kincaid.

"That chicken snake won't be getting any more of our baby chicks. Matt and Memo took care of that. It's been stealing them around here for the longest time, but I never could catch it," said Uncle Wash.

"How do snakes take baby chicks?" asked Em, looking up at him questioningly.

"I'll bet the boys can answer that for you," he replied, nodding his head at Matt and Memo.

Naturally, Matt jumped at the chance to show off more of his knowledge. "Snakes swallow their food whole because their teeth are needle sharp and are not any good for chewing. The bones of their lower jaws are so loosely connected to each other and to the skull, they can separate their jaws wide enough to swallow something two or three times as thick as their own heads."

"That's right," broke in Memo. "One time Papa Jonathan killed a big old diamondback that had a little cottontail halfway swallowed. We rescued that little rabbit and it hopped away into the woods." A pleased smile spread across his face as he remembered.

Apparently Matt had exhausted his wealth of information on snakes because the conversation began to lag. Em felt almost relieved when Uncle Wash and Mr. Kincaid turned the talk to trouble with the Mexican government. That topic was not good either, but the subject of snakes was worse.

"It's not enough that the government won't give us any protection from Indian raids. Now they're sending up Mexican convicts to be pardoned and settle right around us. Since they've stopped allowing us to trade with the United States, the prices on goods brought in from Mexico have soared so that we can hardly afford to buy what we need just to keep going. And did you ever stop to think that there's not one civil court in all of Texas territory?" Uncle Wash asked with disgust. Suddenly he leaped to his feet and began to pace back and forth.

Uncle Wash could always get pretty riled up about things. What amused Em was that he had stirred up Matt and Memo in the meantime. There they sat on the edge of the porch with their jaws set and their eyes glaring.

"Everything you said is true, Wash. If it comes right down to it, I don't believe there's a single man in the settlements who wouldn't take up arms against the Mexican government because I figure there's not a man among us who didn't have the same feeling we did when we reached Texas territory and saw what's here. I can still see those oceans of waving grasses we crossed — the big and little bluestem, Indian grass, and buffalo grass just to mention a few. And the wildlife! Why, the woods are full of badgers, civets, coyotes, deer, foxes, 'possums, rabbits, wild turkeys, and prairie chickens. And just think of the forests of pine, post oak, liveoak, cedar, and elm. It would be an awful thing to have to give up all of this," said Mr.

Kincaid, twirling the ends of his handlebar mustache between his fingers.

"But if you'll just stop and think a minute, the Mexican government might have good reason not to trust the settlers," he added. "The planters have blatantly ignored the government's stand against slavery, the settlers have refused to pay taxes, and most of us have ignored their religious requirement to be Roman Catholics. Then to top it all off, the American government has offered to buy the province. I think the Mexicans believe that if they don't sell Texas to the United States, they will lose it anyway. They're obsessed with the idea that they're losing control, and for that reason they're trying to stop further American immigration into Texas."

"Somebody's coming, Uncle Wash," interrupted Em. She pointed to the two riders moving up the trail toward the cabin.

"It's Uncle Anson! Looks like he found the doctor," said Matt.

Uncle Wash stepped from the porch to meet them. He shook the hand of the portly, middle-aged doctor and then ushered him into the cabin. Uncle Anson drew up a chair and sat down beside Mr. Kincaid.

"Well, now, this must be Miss Cartwright," he said, smiling down at Em.

"No, Mr. Johnson. You're supposed to call me Em."

"Not unless you call me Uncle Anson," he replied. "All the young'uns up and down this river call me Uncle Anson and they call my wife Aunt Molly. We don't answer to anything else. You hear?" Chuckling, he tweaked her ear.

"Yes, sir," she replied. "I would like that very much. I call Cassie's mama and papa Aunt Martha and Uncle Karl, and Cassie calls mine Aunt Miriam and Uncle Zeb. We're no kin, either."

She could already tell she was going to love this tall, stoop-shouldered man with the graying temples. Right now, though, she was worried about him. As soon as the

31

men got well into their discussion about the Mexican government, she had a chance to speak to Matt and Memo about it.

Leaning close, she spoke softly. "Does Uncle Anson have a sore foot? He walks like it hurts him."

"Naw, he got that limp a long time ago," replied Matt.

"A water moccasin popped him on the leg when he scouted Indians for Stephen Austin down on Buffalo Bayou," added Memo. "We'll have to get him to tell you about that sometime."

Oh, no! That awful subject again! Em was not sure at all that she even wanted to hear Uncle Anson's story. She shivered.

About the time Matt opened his mouth to say something — Em figured it was another gruesome snake tale — the doctor and Mama joined them. Sudden silence fell over the porch, and all eyes turned to the doctor.

"He's got several broken ribs and some bad bruises. I didn't see any signs of internal bleeding, which is extremely good news. I would say he's a mighty lucky man. If he had been an inch closer to that mule's hind legs, the injury could have been fatal. No worse than it is, though, it'll still take several weeks for him to recover from this." Turning to Mama and Uncle Wash, he continued, "Make certain he doesn't lift anything. As a matter of fact, he's not to lift a finger around this place for at least a month, then we'll see. Remember that this is very important, or there could be complications."

"We will! We will! We'll do *all* the work," blurted Em excitedly.

Uncle Wash chuckled and looked at Mama knowingly. "Em, your mother and I made a few plans for you earlier today. Cassie made me promise that as soon as you arrived I'd take you over there for a visit."

"But what about Papa? Don't you need me to help take care of him?" she asked, looking at her mother.

"Now, just let me finish," said Uncle Wash, waving

32

her into silence. "Uncle Anson has already said that Aunt Molly is planning to come and help."

For an instant her eyes brightened in anticipation of seeing Cassie, but then they clouded again. What if Papa — no, she would not allow such a thought to enter her mind.

Mama must have sensed her dilemma. "Honey, you go right on over there and spend a couple of days with Cassie and have a very good time. Don't you worry an instant about Papa. Aunt Molly and I will take very, very good care of him while you're gone. He'll be just fine," she said reassuringly.

"Aunt Molly is mighty good at taking care of sick folks," added Uncle Anson.

"Wash, I've been sittin' here thinkin'," Mr. Kincaid said. "To save you the trip, Matt and Memo can ride over there with Em. They've sat around here until they're about to get fidgety and miserable with nothing to do. I'm positive they'd be more than glad to ride over to the Waggoners with Em."

Well, Em wasn't at all positive about that when she glanced over at the boys and saw the distraught looks on their faces. She almost giggled aloud. It was obvious they were less than enthusiastic about this mission. With shoulders drooping and heads down, they slowly slid from the porch and plodded across the yard toward their horses.

"Em, you take my horse. Uncle Anson and I will wait right here until you boys get back. Don't tarry long, now. We've got chores to do at home before nightfall," warned Mr. Kincaid.

"You can rest easy about that, Pa," said Matt, stressing each word with a shake of his head.

"Sure can, Papa Jonathan," chimed in Memo. "We'll be back here *way* before dark. As soon as we get there, we'll probably turn right around and head back. More than likely won't even get down off our horses, will we,

Matt?" Poor Matt was too absorbed in his own dismal thoughts to even answer.

In short order, Em and the boys were on the trail to the Waggoner place. As they moved along, Matt and Memo were locked in somber silence until finally Em heard Matt mumbling something under his breath about Cassie. She covered her mouth to muffle a giggle.

6

Cassie

"Well! Things just can't be all *that* bad. What's the matter with you two? You haven't said a single word since we left the cabin," said Em, finally breaking the brooding silence.

"Thinkin'," muttered Matt dispiritedly.

"Me too," said Memo glumly.

"Thinking about what?" she asked, pretending she did not already know what was pressing hard on their minds. A sly, mischievous smile hovered around her mouth.

"I'm just thinkin' that I'd better warn Memo. We've got to be *awful* careful," he said, giving Memo a sidelong glance and shaking his head in dead seriousness.

"Awful careful of what?" asked Em, continuing to act innocent.

"Careful that Cassie doesn't trick us into some kind of contest — that's what." Matt blinked his big blue eyes and frowned in nervous apprehension.

"Aw, she'll have to work fast if she does that. Remember? Papa Jonathan told us not to tarry," Memo reminded him.

"Oh, yeah," drawled Matt, looking much happier about the entire state of affairs. He set his jaw firmly and settled his hat tighter on his head as if he were now ready for anybody or anything.

A moment before they rode into the clearing within sight of the Waggoner cabin, a savage, blood-curdling screech ripped the air right above their heads. The crazed horses reared, almost sending their terrified charges toppling to the ground. *Ker-plop!* A form dropped from the branches above them and landed on the horse with Matt. Em glimpsed wild-eyed Matt grappling in desperation to free himself from the clutching arms encircling his waist. Despite the panic of the moment, she recognized that mop of fiery-red hair.

"Cassie!" she squealed.

"Em!" shrieked Cassie.

They both slid to the ground and ran into each other's arms, laughing, hugging, and dancing around, completely oblivious to all else about them. After several crazy moments, sanity finally set in — that is, as much sanity as was possible with Cassie around.

"When did you get here, Em? And where are Uncle Zeb and Aunt Miriam? What are you doing with Matt and Memo?"

"You scared us out of a year's growth," said Em, drawing a deep breath. "First, I want you to tell me how you happened to be up in that tree."

"Well, you see, I took Daddy some fresh drinking water to the field. On my way back to the house I heard someone coming through the woods. With all the talk nowadays about war, *banditos,* Comanches, and Mexican convicts, I figured if you were enemy, I'd be ready to give you a hard time with this slingshot," she said, yanking the weapon from her waist. She whizzed it above her head and pretended to release a shot toward Matt. He ducked and she howled with laughter. Straightening quickly and sitting stiffly in the saddle, he looked quite

36

exasperated while Memo sat in his usual state of wide-eyed, speechless wonder.

"Come on," said Em, motioning to them. "Let's walk the rest of the way with Cassie."

With reluctance, they eased from their saddles. As they strolled toward the cabin, Em told Cassie about the accident. Cassie looked very sad until Em told her she had come to visit for a couple of days. Then she burst out with a loud whoop and did a couple of cartwheels. The boys stood aside, giving her wide berth.

"Let's go tell Daddy about Uncle Zeb," said Cassie, wiping her gritty hands on her buckskins.

They left their horses at the edge of the field and started across the neatly plowed furrows, sinking ankle-deep into the soft, broken soil. Em smothered a giggle when she noticed that Matt and Memo kept their eyes peeled on Cassie, watching her suspiciously as if they anticipated some outlandish prank at any moment. They seemed determined to be prepared.

"They're perfect — just *perfect!*" exclaimed Cassie. Her eyes, popping with deviltry, scanned the freshly plowed ground. A ghost of a smile twitched the corners of her mouth. Instantly Matt and Memo snapped to full attention.

"What's perfect?" asked Em.

"The clods, silly. Those beautiful dirt clods," Cassie replied, grinning mischievously. She stooped to scoop into her hand one of the moist, firmly packed clumps of earth.

Matt gasped loudly, took a giant leap into the air, then tore across the field as fast as his long, clumsy legs would carry him. Memo floundered back and forth, not seeming to know what to do nor which way to go. He finally stood still and looked desperate. As it happened, he had little need for concern since Cassie obviously preferred the moving target. Her aim was true.

The dirt clod caught Matt squarely on the back, disintegrating into a million tiny particles. He froze in his tracks for a moment. Then scooping up a clod, he wheeled around and sailed it toward Cassie. With each exchange, the contest gained momentum. Matt was thoroughly caught up in the rhythm of dodging and throwing, dodging and throwing. But somehow in the heat of competition, he got off tempo. He saw it coming too late to duck but in time for his mouth to form an untimely, automatic "oh." He let his dirt clod plop to the ground, and he began to spit and sputter.

"Cassie! What in the world is goin' on here? You cut that out right now!" roared her father, interrupting her release of another well-aimed missile. All eyes turned in his direction — except, of course, for Matt's. He was still in the process of trying to see at all. "What am I goin' to do with you — always treatin' Matt the way you do!" he scolded. Then he spied Em. "Well! Little Em! When did you get here?" he asked, giving her a big hug.

"Daddy, I'm so excited! Em's come to visit for a couple of days. But I'm sad too. Uncle Zeb's hurt. Old Jake kicked him in the stomach. The doctor says he'll get well, but it'll take several weeks."

"Zeb's hurt!" exclaimed Uncle Karl worriedly. "I've got to go see about him." He quickly unhitched the mules from the plow and handed the reins to Cassie. "Turn them loose in the lot and tell your mother where I've gone. Em, I'll just take the horse you rode and worry later about how I'll get home."

"Memo and I will ride with you," said Matt quickly. "Come on, Memo. Let's go." They took to a run across the field toward their horses as if they could hardly wait to get on the trail.

" 'Bye, Matt. 'Bye, Memo. Thanks for coming with me," called Em. They turned and waved to her then vaulted onto their horses and streaked away with Uncle Karl.

7

A Brush with Banditos

"Mama, with Rachel facing me across the table, it's awfully hard to try to eat anything and enjoy it. Just *look* at her! She's *got* to be the messiest baby in the whole world when she eats," said Cassie, crinkling her nose. "Aw, *Mama*! She's even got it in her *eyelashes!*" she groaned, making a big production by turning her head and squeezing her eyes tightly shut.

Eighteen-month-old Rachel had both tiny fists full of molasses-soaked flapjacks and was attempting to stuff every crumb into her mouth at once. The sticky food covered her face and made strings of her hair.

"Well, if you and Em will see that the others wash their hands, I'll see if there's any possible way to get this child clean." Aunt Martha heaved a helpless sigh. "I don't know where to start first. It's a puzzle just to try to figure out a way to pick her up without getting flapjacks and molasses all over me too." The children giggled.

After Rachel was bathed from head to toe, Aunt Martha shooed her and the other children out the door to play in the front yard. Cassie launched into stacking the dishes, making such a clatter that Aunt Martha winced and shook her head. Although every dish was in immediate peril in the hands of Cassie, Aunt Martha seemed determined that her reckless daughter *would* learn to do some of the chores around the house with more delicacy.

"Let's make short work of this, Em. We've got lots better ways to spend our time today before Uncle Wash comes to take you home," said Cassie, moving about the kitchen like a whirling tornado. "I wish you didn't have to go today. Seems like you just got here."

"I know," said Em, "but I really am anxious about Papa. Even though Uncle Karl has gone every day to check on him and thinks he is getting better, I can't wait to see for myself."

Cassie got the big pan of dishwater ready and fell to her work in earnest. She gathered up a stack of dishes and dumped them into the soapy water. She swiped, she mopped, she sloshed, and she slung water until the front of her buckskins was soaked and she stood in a pool on the floor. Each time Em reached for a dish to dry, she s-t-r-e-t-c-h-e-d her arm as far as she could, keeping out of the way of the tidal wave in the dishpan. Occasionally she stopped to hold her sides that ached from laughing so hard at Cassie's harum-scarum performance.

"You can learn how to do all these sissy things that you want, but you need to face facts, Em," said Cassie. "Women and girls have got the raw deal out here. They have to spend long, tedious hours cooking, cleaning house, making and pouring soap, molding tallow candles in cane stalks, tending the garden, feeding the animals, caring for children — doing all the deadly boring chores in and around the house while the men and boys get to go hunting, fishing, and riding the prairies. Shucks! That's what I'd rather do any old day." Then she leaned and whispered to Em so Aunt Martha could not hear. "You'd better take my advice and play ignorant as long as you can."

Em giggled. She figured Aunt Martha was fighting a losing battle with Cassie at this point. She didn't know which would prove to be more durable — the dishes or Aunt Martha's nerves — before the last plate was dried and safely in its place on the shelf.

"Come on, Em," whispered Cassie, pulling her by the hand.

They crept down the trail toward the river for a short distance then stopped to peer from behind a liveoak to see if any of the children were following. They had made good their escape, and Em could see the reason for it. The children were entirely too busy to even notice them. Nine-year-old Joe dangled upside down, swinging by his legs from the spindly branch of a tree. Six-year-old Maggie clutched a half-drowned kitten in her small hands, poised to baptize its sins away just one more time in the rain barrel. Georgie, hardly more than a baby himself, strained and tottered as he lugged Rachel around the yard with his arms locked tightly around her chest. Amanda, the eight-year-old little lady of the family, was up to her elbows in mud pies.

Aunt Martha stuck her head out the door to check on their activities. Her strong voice carried through the woods. "Joe! Get down out of that tree this instant before you fall and break your neck! Maggie, put that poor little kitten down. You're going to drown it if you dunk it one more time! Amanda, get Rachel away from Georgie before he falls with her. And don't let her eat any of those mud pies!"

Em giggled. She *loved* it! Seldom was there a quiet moment in the Waggoner household until all of the children were snug in their beds and fast asleep. Although pure and simple bedlam reigned, Em cherished every moment with the happy family.

"Come on before they miss us," whispered Cassie urgently.

They skipped hand-in-hand down the well-worn trail. Em pulled back when she spied a little bushy-tailed tree squirrel resting on its hind legs under an old oak. The squirrel was holding an acorn in its tiny front feet.

The girls stood motionless, scarcely daring to breathe. For several moments they watched it nibble, nibble. Finally Cassie, having remained still longer than normal for her, made a slight move. The frightened little animal scampered up the tree, spreading its legs straight out and leaping from limb to limb. It finally skittered into a hole far up the trunk.

They continued down the leaf-strewn trail aflame with fall's rich colors of red and gold. Suddenly Cassie stopped at the foot of a huge tree whose branches sagged heavily with ripening walnuts.

"This must be where you get your ammunition for your slingshot," said Em.

"Yep, and it's also where I come to get away all by myself," she replied, turning her face skyward and looking up into the tall branches. "It's probably where I'll hide out the next time Mama mentions books to me too. She started in on that subject as soon as she met Mrs. Kincaid. She tried to send me over to have lessons with Matt and Memo, but I begged her to let me wait until you got here so we could go together. I hope she's forgotten all about it by now. Who wants to be all cooped up tryin' to learn to read and write and do 'rithmetic? What I really need to do is practice using this slingshot if we're goin' to have to fight the Mexicans."

"What about Memo? He is Mexican. Will we have to fight him too?" Em asked.

"Of course not, silly. Memo's one of us even if he is Mexican. His family settled in Texas just like we did, and his father didn't like how the Mexican government treats the settlers either. Who in the world could ever fight somebody like Memo? He thinks I'm crazy, but I like him anyway. Now, don't you go and tell him. I'm supposed to hate boys, you know. But he's different — so polite and all."

"Don't you like Matt?" Em asked.

"Well — ," said Cassie, squinting her eyes and wrinkling her forehead as if she were truly undecided about the matter.

"Well, don't you?" Em prodded her.

"You'll have to promise to keep it a deep, dark secret forever and ever," said Cassie.

"I will. I promise, Cassie. Just tell me."

"Well . . . I like him," she whispered, as if she were afraid for even the squirrels and birds to hear. "But what I like most of all about Matt is the way I can tease him 'til he gets so bumfuzzled he can't remember his own name. That's more fun than eatin' worms," she answered with a giggle. "But let's get off the subject of boys. Come on and climb to the top of this tree with me. You can see the whole world from up there."

She grasped the frayed piece of rope that dangled from a limb and pulled herself along as she walked up the trunk. In a moment she was looking down at Em from the lower branch.

"Come on up. It's easy."

Em leaned her head far back and gazed high into the branches. The tip-top limbs looked as if they reached all the way to the heavens.

"You go ahead. It's no problem for you in those buck-skins, but I don't think I want to try it in these long skirts," she replied.

Just then from far out in the woods came a lonesome, mournful cry. *Whip-poor-will! Whip-poor-will!* A chill ran up and down Em's spine. Wide-eyed, she gazed up at Cassie.

"What a crazy, mixed-up bird," said Cassie with a puzzled look. "I've never heard the cry of a whippoorwill except at night. During the day they usually just sit around on the ground or on a log and rest. Something must have disturbed it." She shrugged her shoulders slightly in an unconcerned way and then motioned to Em with a wave of her arm. "Grab that rope and come on up here with me."

It was very lonely at the foot of that old tree. Perhaps

43

climbing up a few branches would not be too difficult. Feeling an uncontrollable urge to be near someone, Em struggled with the rope and her long skirts until she finally worked her way up the trunk. Cassie pulled her onto the limb.

"Watch me. I can get to the top faster than Matt Kincaid ever could," said Cassie, starting her ascent to the dizzying heights. Within seconds, she was looking down from the topmost branch.

Em maneuvered her way carefully from limb to limb. When she was halfway up the tree, the rustle of leaves and the crackle of dry twigs caught her ear. Cassie apparently heard it too, for she made not a single sound. Em's heart pounded in her chest. Terror held her frozen to the limb. When three riders moved into view amidst the squeak of leather, she turned as weak as a newborn kitten and felt faint. After what seemed an agonizing eternity, the horses moved past the tree. The men turned their heads, scanning the woods in all directions as if they were searching for something or someone. Had they heard her and Cassie talking? They moved slowly ahead, finally disappearing into the woods. For several minutes the girls sat like stones, not daring to move nor make a sound. Then Cassie slipped down the tree until she reached Em.

"Mexican *banditos,*" she whispered, putting her mouth close to Em's ear. "I wonder what they're doing in these woods."

"I don't know, but we'd better get to the cabin as fast as we can and tell Aunt Martha," replied Em.

"Oh, no! We can't tell Mama. She'd never let me come down here again by myself, and I just couldn't bear that. This is my very favorite place in the whole world. Please don't say a word about this, Em. Those *banditos* were just passing through and probably won't ever come back this way again. Besides, if they do come back, I can take care of them in short order with my slingshot. These walnuts make the best shot you ever saw. They're even

The men turned their heads, scanning the woods in all directions.

better than rocks. I'll betcha I could knock the eye out of a gnat with this thing," she said.

"Well, for heaven's sake don't try it now," warned Em.

They waited several more minutes. Then as noiselessly as they could manage, they made their way to the ground and flew up the path to the cabin. Em felt uncomfortably guilty about not telling Aunt Martha. But maybe Cassie was right. Perhaps those *banditos* would never return.

When they bounded breathlessly through the kitchen doorway, Aunt Martha scolded, "Cassie, I've been calling and calling for you. Why didn't you answer?"

"I didn't hear you, Mama. Did you hear her, Em?"

"No, Aunt Martha. I didn't hear you either."

"I do hope you're not wandering too far away from the house," she said with a warning glance at Cassie. Then she shrugged. "Oh, well, maybe you two were so busy talking, you couldn't hear me. Anyway, I'm glad you're back now. I'd like for you to grind some corn for pone. I've an idea it might taste pretty good with this stew. Em, if your Uncle Wash happens to get here in time, he can eat with us. He has always seemed to enjoy my stew."

Aunt Martha leaned over the hearth, lifted the lid from the steaming pot, and stirred briskly with the long-handled wooden spoon. A savory aroma filled the kitchen.

"U-m-m!" I *know* he would like that," said Em. "It smells so good I can hardly wait, Aunt Martha."

Any chore in the out-of-doors suited Cassie perfectly. "Come on, Em," she said, taking an empty pail from a peg near the door and heading for the patch near the house to get some of the corn that had been left to harden on the stalk. As they pulled each ear, they stripped away the husks.

When the pail was filled to brimming, they carried it back to the house to grate the corn. The grater they used was an old coffee pot Uncle Karl had flattened, punched full of small holes, then shaped into an oval and fastened to a board. They poured the grated corn into a mortar Uncle Karl had made from a stump he hollowed out by burning and scraping. Taking turns, they pulverized the corn into meal with a pestle that was fastened to a long pole resting in the fork of a tree. Em worked until she was breathless, then Cassie grabbed the end of the pole and swung it in an up-and-down motion, forcing the pestle to come down hard into the hollow stump to crush the corn.

As always, the younger children were as close to Cassie's elbow as they could get. They stood watching every stroke of the pestle. She brought the pole down with a mighty swish. Joe yelped and fell to the ground, holding his head. Rachel and Georgie, frightened by the sudden outburst, filled the air with deafening shrieks while Maggie and Amanda jigged up and down in a panic, wringing their hands. With terror-filled eyes, Aunt Martha burst from the cabin and ran across the yard to Joe. She gathered him into her arms and carried him into the house, leaving Cassie and Em to calm the little ones.

After examining his wound and discovering that the skin was hardly broken, Aunt Martha breathed a ragged sigh of relief. She held him close and wiped at his tears with her apron.

"You'll be fit as a fiddle in no time. I know it hurts, but it's only a scratch. I'll put a poultice of mud and oak juice on it and by morning you won't even know it was ever there. I knew Amanda's mud pies were surely good for something. She works so hard at making them," she said with a chuckle. When Joe managed a weak smile through his tears, they all broke into giggles and laughter, relieved that he was not badly wounded.

Soon the household was back to its natural state of bedlam without disaster. Somehow Aunt Martha had finished preparing the noon meal. Uncle Wash arrived in time to enjoy some of the delicious stew and corn pone with them. He visited until time for Uncle Karl to return to the field. Then he lifted Em onto the horse with him and they started for home. Em promised Cassie that not many days would pass before they would be together again.

8

Comanche Scare

Em eagerly anticipated seeing much improvement in her father's condition when she reached home. When she saw him, her heart sank. She bowed to the painful fact that if there was any change at all, it was surely not for the better.

In the days that followed, she watched him grow more pale and weak. He could do little more than creep from bed to chair or kitchen table. Since any kind of work around the place was clearly out of the question for him, the neighbors came as often as they could to lend Uncle Wash a helping hand.

A troubled Em could also see the worry lines in Mama's face. How much longer could they watch him waste away right before their very eyes? Em decided that something had to be done — and soon! Thus far, she had been reluctant to mention the old Comanche to Mama and Uncle Wash for fear that they would scoff at the idea. She had no other alternative now. She was ready for Matt and Memo to find him and bring him to work his wonders on Papa.

Realizing that his unannounced arrival might be

less than welcome, she was forced to make a decision. Whom should she tell, Mama or Uncle Wash? She mulled it over carefully in her mind, finally reaching the conclusion that Uncle Wash was her logical choice. After all, didn't he believe in some sort of magic himself? Hadn't he "witched" the well with his divining rod?

One time he had shown her what power the rod had to locate underground water. Taking the forked branch and gripping the two forks firmly in his hands, he bent them forward. The main stem moved up and down as he walked across the ground. When he relaxed his hold and the stem pointed downward, he said it meant that water flowed underground at that point. Mama teased him. She believed common sense about where water is usually found told him to dig their well in the right spot. But his faith remained unaltered. He *believed* in that divining rod!

Em looked down into the dark depths of the well. Whichever it was, Uncle Wash's common sense or his divining rod, made no difference. The end result was what counted. So what difference did it make what the old Comanche used — hocus-pocus or remedies? She did not care so long as it made Papa well.

Her decision was made. She saw Uncle Wash at the far side of the field. Poor Uncle Wash! With steely endurance, day after day he toiled from faint morning light to dusky evening. He was always in a race against time, rushing to clear the fields and get them in shape before the cold winter months arrived.

Although a touch of fall was already in the air, the October sun burned down from the cloudless sky. Em felt sure Uncle Wash was very hot and tired from working Old Jake and figured he might relish a fresh drink from the cool depths of the well. She drew a bucket, filled a small pail, and embarked upon her mission. In the distance she saw Old Jake with powerful hind legs bent, straining and pulling with all his might to remove a deeply embedded stump from the soil while Uncle Wash roared his commands. "Move, Jake! Yow! Git in there, mule! One more time now! That's good, Jake. Steady. Steady."

"Uncle Wash! Uncle Wash!" called Em, hurrying toward him, sloshing water out of the pail in her haste. "I've got a cool drink for you. Wait a minute before you and Jake get started again."

"Well, now! It's awfully nice of you to think of doing that for me," he said, removing his hat. With the sleeve of his shirt, he swabbed the beads of sweat from his brow. She handed him the pail and he drank thirstily. "My! That tasted good — much better than the stale water I brought with me early this morning." He laid an arm across her shoulders and they strolled to the edge of the field to sit down in the shade of an elm.

Uncle Wash leaned his back against the trunk and looked out across the field. "One would think Old Jake senses that time is growing short to finish clearing. Not once today has he shown his stubborn streak and refused to work."

Em only half listened as she pulled thoughtfully at tiny blades of grass that were already beginning to brown and curl from early frost. Life was fading from them just as it was from Papa. What a horrifying thought! She turned urgently to her uncle, her reluctance now a thing of the past.

"Uncle Wash, I need to discuss something with you. I don't think Papa's getting any better, and I'm terribly worried."

"Aw, honey, I think he's some better. At least he's not in as much pain. I'll have to admit, though, he's not improving as fast as we had hoped," he said, shaking his head.

"Well, I've heard of someone who might be able to help him, and I've got an idea."

"Now, just what idea do you have in that little head of yours?" he asked, reaching to tweak her nose.

"Matt and Memo know an old Comanche who — "

Her voice died abruptly when Uncle Wash placed a finger across his lips to shush her. He bounded to his feet. The thrum of hoofbeats moved quickly and steadily nearer. When Em moved to stand close to Uncle Wash, he swept her behind him with his arm. They waited. In a moment the rider burst from the woods, streaking toward them at full speed.

"It's Karl, and it doesn't look like he's come just to visit. Wonder what's happened?" Uncle Wash took several anxious steps toward him.

"Wash!" he called. "The Mexicans! It's started!" When he reached them, he reined his winded horse and swung to the ground.

"Well, what's happened?" asked Uncle Wash anxiously.

"I rode into Gonzales this morning and found everybody in a stew. Some Mexican soldiers tried to seize that little cannon the government gave us for protection against the Indians. The citizens have taken the soldiers as prisoners, but they're expecting more to come. I was asked to spread the word to the neighbors along the river that every able-bodied man is needed in town right away with plenty of load for his gun — at least a hundred rounds.

"Looks like they're tryin' to disarm us," he continued. "If we let that happen, they'll have a free hand to treat us any way they take a notion, and it's bad enough as it is. I've got to be movin' on. I've got a few more stops to make before I head back home. Anson and Jonathan are waiting for me. Come on as soon as you can. We'll meet you in Gonzales at Charlie Cole's store." With that, he climbed back into the saddle, wheeled his horse, and sped away.

Uncle Wash immediately got into motion. He grabbed the reins and clucked his tongue at Old Jake. The old mule stood like stone. Uncle Wash clucked again to deaf ears. Since he was always extremely kind to the animals, Em was shocked when, in his urgent need to make Old Jake move fast, he thwacked him across the firm rump with the reins. Well, it must have really been a stunner for Old Jake. With head held high and ears backed, he stepped so lively that Uncle Wash had to break into a run to stay up with him. Old Jake *trotting*? For a second, Em thought her eyes were deceiving her.

She raced to the cabin to tell Mama and Papa the disturbing news. First there were *banditos*. And now, Mexican soldiers! Living in Texas territory was getting downright scary to her. And as if *banditos* and Mexican soldiers were not enough to frighten a body to death, there was the ever-present threat of a Comanche raid to trouble the mind.

By the time she bounded into the kitchen, she had worked herself into such a dither, she could hardly do more than stammer breathlessly, "Uncle Karl — Uncle Wash — Mexicans!"

"Hold on a minute," said Mama, helping her onto the bench. "Take a deep breath." Em drew air deep into her lungs.

"Now tell me what has you so upset," said Mama calmly.

"Uncle Wash! He's going to fight the Mexicans!"

"What in heaven's name are you talking about, child?" she asked.

"Uncle Karl rode over here to tell Uncle Wash about it. They've got to go into Gonzales right away!"

Before she could explain further, Uncle Wash burst into the kitchen. As quickly as he could, he told Mama and Papa what had happened. "Miriam, if you'll put some food in my knapsack while I gather up some load and my bedroll, I can get on my way."

With the help of Em and Mama, in a few short minutes he was ready to ride. He lifted his gun from the antler rack with one hand and the pouch of arrowheads with the other. Uncle Wash and his arrowheads! He never left the place without them.

The day wore itself into evening. Mama and Em

53

headed for the barn to feed the animals. They took special care to give the wild mustangs in the stock pen plenty of feed.

By the time they started back to the cabin, darkness had closed in. Mama headed straight for the kitchen to prepare the night meal. In a short time venison was sizzling in the old black skillet. She eyed it thoughtfully.

"You know, Em, I believe I'll run out to the smokehouse and get some dried turkey breast. Papa might have more appetite for that since he's already had venison once today."

"I'll get it," said Em, sliding the bar from the door and stepping outside before Mama could stop her.

"I'll stand right here in the doorway until you get back," she called.

As Em crossed the moon-silvered yard, the eerie silence of the clear, starry night made her pulse quicken. The whole world outside seemed lifeless. Not a sound came from the animals, birds, or countless insects. When she reached to slide the bar from the smokehouse door, she found it already ajar. How careless! She made a mental note to tell Mama they must be more careful. Why, an animal could get in there and get all of their meat!

Pulling wide the heavy door, she stepped inside. In the dimness she reached up to get the turkey breast. Her hands suddenly froze in midair. What was it? No sound had caught her ear, but she sensed that she was not alone. Cutting her eyes around and searching the dark shadows, she spied him crouched in a corner. Comanche!

His almost nude body was covered with only a breechcloth of white buckskin. Even in the dimness, she could see the brightly colored tassels that decorated it. Long, jet-black hair fell to his shoulders, and a single feather was thrust into the beaded band around his brow. In his hand he held a bow, and strapped on his coppery back was a horsehide quiver filled with arrows.

He rose quickly and moved toward her in a half crouch. She whirled, picked up her long skirts, and flew toward the cabin. Shrill screams tore from her throat. Mama's welcome arms pulled her into the kitchen. Papa slammed the door and slid the bar across it. Then he sank breathlessly to the kitchen bench and held his gun ready.

Panic-stricken, Em clung to Mama. After a moment that seemed like an eternity, they heard the logs of the stock pen break loose. Horses thundered across the yard. Then there was whooping and hollering of what sounded like at least a half dozen Comanche braves.

"There go the mustangs and there's not a thing we can do," said Papa with eyes blazing. The muscles in his jaws rippled as he clenched his teeth. Though he was weak and in pain, he rose from the bench and snatched the hunting horn from the antler rack.

"Miriam, please open that door for me," he said in a voice shaking with rage.

"What are you going to do?" asked Mama anxiously.

"All I *can* do. Try to warn the neighbors," he replied.

Em and Mama helped him down the steps and into the front yard. Lifting the hunting horn and turning it to the open sky, he blew two long *"ahloos."* The tones swelled over the countryside. When the echoes faded, he raised the gun and fired into the star-strewn heavens. Having done all he could do to warn those within hearing distance that Comanches were on the prowl, he turned wearily. Em and Mama helped him up the steps and back into the cabin.

"They must have known most of the men are in Gonzales and that the women and children are left alone. Martha and those six children . . . if I thought I could make it, I'd go over there and see about them," he said, sinking to the bench, pale and exhausted.

"Now, Zeb, that's out of the question. Right now, all we can do is hope and pray those Comanches got what they wanted here and will leave others alone," said Mama.

Despair settled down upon Em. She could not think

of anything but Aunt Martha and the children! What awful thing could be happening to them at this very moment? Sick at heart, she finally curled up on the pallet Mama had spread for her next to their bed and pulled the covers over her head in a vain attempt to blot out the terrifying thoughts that whirled and spun in her head.

9

Uncle Wash
Rides Away

The night was heavy with tension. The hours seemed to crawl. In the stillness, Em's ears were acutely attuned to the slightest sound — the whisper of the wind, the rustle of the leaves, the occasional call of the night bird.

Troubled thoughts rolled and tumbled in her head. Would the Comanches return? Had they raided the Waggoner place? What was happening to Uncle Wash? She rolled and tossed on the pallet with a million terrifying thoughts running through her mind. In the wee hours of the morning, she finally gave in to total fatigue and closed her eyes.

Mama's stirring wrenched her into wakefulness while it was still pitch dark. She sat bolt upright on her pallet and rubbed her burning eyes with her fists. For one disoriented moment she could not remember where she was because she had not awakened in her cozy bed in the loft. Then memory of the horrors of the night came flooding back.

"What is it?" she asked anxiously when she heard the bar sliding from the door.

"Nothing, honey. It's morning and I'm going to the

kitchen to cook us some breakfast. You and Papa doze a while longer, and I'll call you when it's ready," came Mama's soothing voice.

Em lay back on the pallet and closed her eyes, but awful memories of the night clogged her mind and sleep refused to take her. Finally, with an impatient sigh, she jumped up, rushed over and planted a good-morning kiss on Papa's cheek, and headed for the kitchen. When she stepped into the dog-trot, she saw the first hint of light graying the eastern horizon. For a moment she stood and breathed deeply the crisp, cool, open air. She then hurried in to help Mama with breakfast.

"Couldn't sleep, honey?"

"No, Mama."

"Well, breakfast is about ready, anyway. Would you put the molasses on the table and then go tell Papa the flapjacks are almost done?"

Flapjacks! Em's heart plummeted to her feet at the thought. Of all the mornings to have flapjacks, why did it have to be this one? But how could Mama know? Em set the molasses on the table and with doleful steps she plodded across the dog-trot to tell Papa.

As they sat around the cheerless table, very few words passed between them. Em almost choked on each bite she put in her mouth. Finally she gave up and shoved her plate away.

"Mama, it's not that your flapjacks aren't delicious as always. It's just that I have no appetite for them. They remind me too much of little Rachel."

"Flapjacks remind you of little Rachel?" she asked.

"The last breakfast I ate with them, we had flapjacks and you should have seen her. She had them smeared from head to toe. Oh, Mama! I'm so worried about Aunt Martha and the children." Papa and Mama exchanged sorrowful glances.

By the time breakfast was over and the dishes were washed and put away, gray dawn had changed to a radiant, sunlit morning. What a gloriously beautiful day it might be if only it bore good news.

Em fumed and fretted all morning. Soon after the hour of noon, Uncle Wash rode in, looking weary but safe and sound.

"Uncle Wash!" cried Em when he stepped into the kitchen. "I'm so glad you're back. We've been worried to death about you, and about Aunt Martha and the children since those Comanches came through here last night."

"Comanches!" he exclaimed, turning to Mama with a start.

"Yes, Wash, they came through here last night and stole the mustangs. That was apparently all they wanted because they didn't try to harm us. We've been very concerned about Martha and the children. They may have raided their place too."

He sighed heavily and dropped to the bench. Papa shuffled into the room.

"I'm sorry about the mustangs, Wash," he said.

"Don't be. The main thing is they didn't harm anyone," he replied. "I've got to go see about Martha and the children. None of us will rest easy until we know."

"Let me go with you," pleaded Em.

He turned to Mama. "What do you think, Miriam?"

"I heard her turning and tossing restlessly all during the night. I think she couldn't bear your leaving without her."

"Let's go," he said, grabbing Em by the hand. He lifted her into the saddle and climbed on behind her.

"What happened in Gonzales?" called Mama. "We plain forgot to ask."

"I'll tell you when we get back," replied Uncle Wash over his shoulder.

On the way, Em pursued the subject. "What happened in Gonzales, Uncle Wash?"

"We filled that little cannon with slugs, and with one blast those Mexicans high-tailed it back to Bexar. I figure it's just a matter of time before real trouble starts with them. By the way, Matt and Memo sneaked away from home and were in on that fracas. Jonathan couldn't believe his eyes when they showed up. Memo thinks he must fight the Mexicans in his father's place."

"Why would he want to fight his own people?"

"You see, his family came to Texas to claim land just like we did. His father was also displeased with the way the Mexican government has treated the settlers. Memo comes from a very fine family. They were good neighbors to all of us along the river. We were saddened by the death of those good people. There's not a family along this river that wouldn't have taken Memo just like the Kincaids did."

They talked on until the Waggoner place came into view. Em's heart leaped for joy when she saw the children at their usual play in the front yard.

From the doorway of the cabin, Aunt Martha lifted her arm in greeting. "Howdy, Wash. We certainly didn't expect to see you and Em so soon. Is anything wrong?" she asked.

"No, we've been worried about you and the children and came to check on you. Last night Comanches came roaring by our place and stole the mustangs. Did they come by here?"

"Haven't seen hide nor hair of anybody," she replied. The children were all eyes and ears as they listened.

"Look! Somebody's comin' and they're in an awful hurry," said Cassie, pointing to the rider tearing toward them at top speed.

"It's John Collins. Something must have happened," said Uncle Wash.

Mr. Collins slid from the saddle. "Wash, I'm sure glad you're here. Where's Karl?" he asked breathlessly.

"I'll get him," said Aunt Martha. "He went straight to bed as soon as he got home." She hurriedly disappeared into the house.

In only a moment Uncle Karl stepped out the door,

pulling on his shirt. "What's happened?" he asked, looking sleepily from Uncle Wash to Mr. Collins. The wide-eyed children hovered close.

"I've come to tell you Stephen Austin has put out the word that it's full war this time and we're not laying down our guns until every Mexican soldier is driven out of Texas. He's raising a force to head out for Bexar. Got it in his mind that we're going to take it from the Mexicans. The men are gathering in Gonzales to ride out," he said.

"Do Jonathan and Anson know about this?" asked Uncle Karl.

"No, I haven't made it over there yet," he replied.

"Give me a few minutes and I'll go with you," said Uncle Karl. "Martha, help me get things together." Turning to Uncle Wash, he said, "This kinda puts you between a rock and a hard place with Zeb in his condition. I hope you don't feel that you have to go with us. Why don't you just stay at home and take care of things around there?"

"I wouldn't feel right about that at all. And besides, Zeb is going to feel bad enough that he can't go. It would just make him feel worse if I didn't go because of him. No, I'll take Em on back home and meet you in Gonzales as soon as I can," he said.

"Wash, I see you didn't even stay home long enough today to put away your bedroll and knapsack," said Aunt Martha. "Since you've got them with you, I'll fill your knapsack along with Karl's and you can leave from here with him and John. The children and I will see that Em gets home. Maybe I can talk Zeb and Miriam into coming over here to stay with us while you're gone."

"Martha, I appreciate that, but I don't want to put you and the children in danger of running into those Comanches on the way over there," said Uncle Wash.

"Pshaw! We won't run into any Comanches. They're long gone. They would have already come through here if they intended to. I'll take a gun and we'll be just fine."

"I've got my slingshot too. I'm runnin' low on wal-

61

nuts, but I can use stones if I have to," said Cassie confidently.

"What do you think, Karl?" asked Uncle Wash.

"I think Martha's right. Those Comanches got what they were after last night and left for their camp," he replied.

"That's settled, then," said Aunt Martha. "Give us a minute and we'll have you ready to leave with Karl and John."

Em and Cassie scurried around, helping Aunt Martha fill the knapsacks with food. Soon the men were ready to ride. When Em hugged Uncle Wash goodbye, she heard the clink of arrowheads in the pouch strapped across his shoulder. He turned and looked back at her as he rode away. Suddenly Em got a sick, empty feeling in her stomach. She could not pull her eyes away until he disappeared from view. For a fleeting moment, she felt a darkness without end — no promise of dawn. Then it was gone.

"Cassie, you and Em please go round up the mules down in the pasture while I get things together so we can leave right away. Bring them to the barn lot, but don't try to harness them and hitch them to the wagon. I'll do that myself. Be as quick as you can. Zeb and Miriam are sitting over there worrying their heads off about us," said Aunt Martha.

"Yes, Mama. Come on, Em," she said, heading for the barn. She found two ropes for leading the mules and they hurried toward the pasture down by the river. They rushed along for a ways, and then suddenly Cassie veered off in another direction.

"What are you doing, Cassie?" asked Em, stopping cold in her tracks.

"We're going to take a little detour here. It won't take but a few minutes and it might save our lives. I need another supply of walnuts for my slingshot. Got to be ready in case we come upon something unexpectedly in the woods on the way to your house."

"Aw, come on, Cassie. Can't you use rocks this time?" begged Em. She dreaded going back to that tree.

"Now, silly, I *told* you walnuts are better than rocks any day. They're all about the same size and fit my slingshot perfectly. Not true about rocks. You have to hunt for the right size, and they're scarce as hens' teeth. Don't you see? It'll save time in the long run."

"Well, let's make it quick," said Em, giving in reluctantly and following her.

10

Captured!

"Hurry, Cassie!" called Em as she stood at the foot of the old tree.

"Be down in a second," she replied from her perch on a limb that already drooped with its heavy load of walnuts.

Em almost jumped right out of her skin when she heard the snap of a dry twig. Jerking her head around, she scanned the woods in all directions.

"Please hurry, Cassie. I don't like it here," she moaned.

"Okay, I'm almost finished," Cassie called.

About the time Em started scolding herself for being such a fraidy-cat, large brown hands that seemed to come out of nowhere grabbed her, pinning her arms to her sides. A scream welled in her throat, but only a hoarse whisper escaped her lips. She twisted, she turned, she lunged, and she kicked, but her efforts were futile. She felt like a helpless animal caught in a trap when she realized that three *banditos* held her fast.

Suddenly from up above came the thrashing of leaves. Then a rain of walnuts fell upon their heads. The startled *banditos* released Em and darted for cover. Em heard the *whir-r-r-r, whir-r-r-r* of Cassie's slingshot. One of the *banditos* yelped loudly and grabbed his arm before he disappeared behind a tree. Walnuts whizzed through the air thick and fast. All at once the barrage ceased and Cassie dropped to the ground.

"Run!" screamed Em, tearing up the trail toward the cabin. She felt a breeze as Cassie whisked past her with flying heels that hardly touched the ground. From behind her came the thud of pounding feet getting closer, closer. Blinded with fear, she failed to see the old tree root lying across the trail — one she had leaped over each time they traveled the path. Her toe caught and she pitched headlong to the ground. In an instant Cassie was beside her, pulling her to her feet, but it was too late. The *banditos* surrounded them. Like cornered animals they struggled, but hope was dead.

The scratched, bruised, and blindfolded girls were hoisted onto horses and swept away. After riding for what seemed like forever, the *banditos* reined the horses. Em felt herself being dragged from the horse. When her blindfold was removed and her eyes adjusted to the bright sunlight, she saw Cassie standing nearby squinting and blinking.

"Oh, Cassie!" she cried. "Where are we? What are we going to *do*?"

They stood wrapped in each other's arms and looked all about. There before them was a crude hut, a small one-room affair with a doorway and two irregularly shaped holes for windows. A lean-to constructed of poles and cornstalks was attached to an outside wall. Through the open doorway they saw the hard-packed dirt floor. *Petates,* or straw mats, leaned against the outside wall, sunning in the open air until time to be placed on the floor again for sleeping.

Em's eyes finally came to rest on an old woman under the lean-to, down on her knees before a little bed of glowing coals. On top of the coals lay a piece of sheet iron.

Two tortillas baked on it while her chubby hands prepared another for the griddle. She did not look up but knelt there quietly with a bowl of hulled corn on one side of her and her *metate* on the other. The *metate* was simply two flat stones used for mashing the softened corn into dough. She rolled and patted the dough then tossed it onto the griddle. For the longest time, she kept up the routine like clockwork, taking one tortilla from the griddle, turning another, and putting on the third until she finished.

Slowly she pushed her cumbersome body to her feet and pulled her rebozo, or shawl, snugly about her head. Thick, straight, black hair strung down her back to her waist. Naked feet peeked from beneath her brightly colored full skirts. Her probing black eyes raked Em and Cassie from head to foot while the *banditos* stood with folded arms, looking very pleased with their accomplishment.

Without a word to them, the old woman turned, cupped her hands to her mouth, and screeched, "Rosita! Lupe!"

Shortly two young women rounded the corner of the hut. They might have been considered somewhat handsome had it not been for the greedy gleam in their eyes when they spied Em and Cassie. Time had not played havoc with their fine features and slender bodies as it had the body and face of the old woman. Big smiles of delight spread across their faces, revealing stark-white teeth against dark-brown skin. Dancing around Em and Cassie, they tittered girlishly and then spoke in rapid Spanish to their heroes.

Cassie nudged Em and whispered, "I've learned enough of the language from Memo to understand why they brought us here. We're going to be slaves to their wives. I heard them say something about Coahuila. That's a *long* ways from here. I've heard Daddy talk about it. They're taking us there 'cause they know if they keep us captive here, somebody will come looking for us."

Em's heavy heart sank to the bottom of her feet. With a sickening certainty, she knew Cassie's words rang true. Tears of hopelessness welled in her eyes. Would she ever see Mama and Papa again? What was to be their fate? She shivered uncontrollably.

The *banditos* waved their arms as they issued instructions to their wives. The women rushed to feed the men and gather up their few belongings in and around the hut. After the tortillas and beans were devoured, the oldest *bandito* squatted under the lean-to with eyes locked on Em and Cassie. The two younger men disappeared behind the hut, returning in a few minutes with horses for each of them. Within the hour, they were moving south to Coahuila.

Em recalled what Uncle Wash had said about convicts sent from Mexico to live among the settlers. Now she could fully understand his anger at the Mexican government. She felt certain she and Cassie had fallen victim to members of this undesirable group.

11

Skunk to the Rescue

Coahuila was a land far, far from home. Em and Cassie spent long, miserable days there high in the mountains — captives in the *bandito* camp, slaves to the women. Out of sheer necessity, they learned the language quickly. As long as they jumped to the tasks and performed them to the satisfaction of the women, they were ignored and left to suffer by themselves.

Had weeks passed? Or months? Em had no way of knowing. She could not keep track of time. Each horrible day melted into the next. There they were, locked within the great walls of the Sierra Madres — a place scarcely habitable even for creatures of the wild. One of the giant land barriers in the mountain range, the Tierra Fria where they were held captive, lived up to its name. The temperature hovered at the freezing point during the day, and nights brought a coldness that penetrated to the marrow of the bone.

They took refuge in a deep, dark cave in a steep wall of the mountain. Each night their captors slept in a circle around the small fire that smoldered in the middle of the room. Em and Cassie huddled close for warmth in a dark corner of the cave. Sometimes Em felt she would never be warm again. Oh, what she wouldn't give to be in her cozy bed in the loft of the cabin! Night after miserable night, she awoke often, wishing for morning to come. At least during the days while she and Cassie prepared food for the camp, they could stand near the blazing campfire outside and bask in its warmth.

"Cassie, I'm afraid we'll never see home again," moaned Em in utter despair.

Cassie jerked around with angry eyes flashing and nostrils flaring. "Yes, we *will*! You just wait and see. I've had about all of this slave nonsense I'm going to take!"

"Now, Cassie — "

"Don't 'now Cassie' me! If we don't hurry up and do something to get their attention, they're going to be satisfied to stay here forever making us wait on them hand and foot. I'll tell you something you can depend on for sure. Things are about to start happening around here, 'cause I'm goin' to see that they do. Now hush! Here comes that old woman. Don't say another word," she whispered, turning back to stir the pot of bubbling stew.

The old woman flopped heavily to the straw mat on the ground. She lolled lazily near the fire, warming herself and occasionally dozing when she was not gazing at Em and Cassie with her piercing black eyes. After a time she yawned, sat up straight, and from her pocket drew a tin of snuff. Taking a pinch, she deposited it in her lower lip, exposing her blackened teeth. Em shuddered in revulsion. Although she had witnessed this routine countless times, it was still loathsome to her.

For what seemed an eternity, the woman sat there, leaning occasionally to spit until Em was ready to scream. Finally, with great effort and considerable huffing and puffing, she pushed herself clumsily to her age-stiffened legs and waddled toward the mountain stream nearby. As soon as she was out of earshot, Cassie grabbed Em's arm and pulled her close.

"I thought she'd *never* leave. Keep your eagle eye out

and let me know if you see her coming. I'm going to fix it so they'll *never* want us for cooks again," she whispered through a chuckle.

"Cassie! You're going to get us in a peck of trouble! What crazy stunt are you about to pull?" Em's eyes were wide with alarm.

"You know how they love those hot peppers the old woman doles out to them? Well, I'm going to find them and season this stew like none they have ever tasted before. I think I know where she keeps them. Now, keep your eyes peeled and warn me if you see her coming."

"But the others may come back!" cried Em in desperation.

"They're still tromping around the mountain looking for tomorrow's food. They won't be back for hours. Just do what I say and stand guard for me," she said and hurried into the cave.

Em bit her lower lip and held her breath until she felt her lungs would burst. *Please hurry, Cassie!* she screamed silently. At the precise moment she felt she would literally die of fear, Cassie popped out of the cave holding up a big handful of the fiery-hot chili peppers. With a devilish gleam in her eye, she tossed them one and all into the pot and began to stir vigorously, putting her whole heart and soul into the task of making it the hottest batch of stew they would ever put into their mouths.

"By the time I get through with them, they'll be ready to *take* us back home," said Cassie with resolve.

"Yeah, if they don't kill us first," groaned Em, twitching and turning nervously.

"Do away with their slaves? Uh-uh! The women wouldn't allow it. They've had it too good not having to turn a hand," she replied.

"Well, they'll do *something* to punish us. I *know* they will!" Em moaned.

"We'll worry about that when the time comes," replied Cassie. With a mischievous grin spread across her face, she took the long wooden spoon and ground the floating peppers against the side of the pot, determined that the *banditos* and their wives would get the full effect of each fiery little pod. There was no stopping her now. When Cassie had her mind set, talking to her was like baying to the moon.

When the sun sank behind the mountain wall and the cold night wind increased, the *banditos* and their wives gathered around the campfire for their evening meal. Em found it difficult to hide her anxiety. Her hands trembled so much that she could hardly serve each of them the portions Cassie had ladled into wooden bowls.

Pleased *oh's* and *ah's* arose from the men as they settled down to partake of the meal. Em clenched her fists to disguise the trembling as one by one they eagerly lifted the wooden spoons and slurped big mouthfuls. Instantly, eyes all but popped out of their heads and mouths flew open. Order became chaos. Utensils clattered to the hard ground as they jumped frantically to their feet and headed for the cold water of the mountain stream, fanning their tongues as they ran. Em had never heard such moaning and groaning.

Suddenly panic gripped her. "Cassie! They'll make *us* eat that stew! What are we going to do!" she cried.

"This!" she said, tipping the pot on its side. The contents spilled onto the ground and was immediately swallowed up by the moisture-starved, powdery soil.

Soon relieved of their short-lived suffering, the *banditos* and the two younger women stalked angrily toward Em and Cassie. But the old woman held up a restraining hand with a promise that the two girls would receive their punishment. She was true to her word. That cold, wind-swept night found them huddled together outside the door of the cave, with only their tattered blankets to cover them. They shivered and shook in the frigid wind sweeping down from the peaks and whistling and sighing along the mountain pass. Inside the cave, the *banditos* and their wives slept soundly.

Em jumped like she was shot and clung to Cassie when she heard movement in the clump of bushes near them. What was it? A mountain lion ready to pounce? She and Cassie sat stone still and strained their eyes to see. In a moment a small animal slowly emerged from the dark shadows. The snow-white streak on its back glistened in the radiant moonlight.

The air left Cassie's lungs with a rush. "Thank goodness it's only a little skunk!"

They did not move a muscle as it came toward them, walking slowly and deliberately like a person with shoes too tight. Ignoring them as if they were no more than part of the natural surroundings, it wandered on past them and then stopped at the opening of the cave. Cassie, being her old impulsive self, shot to her feet and shooed it into the cave with the sleeping, unsuspecting victims.

In seconds a rank, vile-smelling odor saturated the air. Em and Cassie buried their noses deep in their blankets.

"You're about to see the action pick up considerably around here," came Cassie's muffled voice from inside the blanket. Her shoulders shook with laughter.

The words were no sooner out of her mouth than they came spilling from the cave, darting wildly here and there. Out of the corner of her eye, Em saw the little skunk tippy-toe daintily through the cave door and disappear into the night. The men and women, in desperation, finally waded into the icy mountain stream to wash away the nauseating scent.

"They don't know much about skunks or they'd know water won't get rid of that odor," said Cassie, still clamping her nose tightly shut.

"What will they do to us now?" fretted Em. "You've got to quit doing things to aggravate them." Still, even with these words of warning, she knew it would be easier

72

to move a mountain than it would be to change Cassie's impulsive nature.

"Don't worry. They can't know but what that little skunk wandered into the cave all by itself without any help from us. I can tell you one thing you can depend on. There are no if's, and's, or but's about it. Get ready to travel, 'cause we'll be clearing out of this place pronto. Nobody, but *nobody,* can live in that cave for a long time to come. I believe even a skunk would turn up its nose in there."

Cassie's prediction held true. In all haste they gathered their belongings. Leaving their remote, safe retreat in the middle of the bitterly cold night, they headed down the rugged mountain trail.

12

March to the Alamo

Leading their horses, they snaked single-file down the narrow, zigzag mountain path. Sometimes they moved gingerly around a cactus or small shrub that partially blocked the trail. Each moved in sullen silence, exchanging not a single word.

Em and Cassie shivered in the bitter cold. The stinging north wind numbed their feet and legs so they did not feel the scraping and tearing of the jagged rocks when they stumbled against them. A place to stop and rest on the treacherous trail seemed nonexistent. For hours they trudged over the rugged, rocky terrain. With every agonizing step, Em felt herself growing weaker.

"Cassie, I can't go any farther," she uttered through chattering teeth.

Cassie took firm hold of her arm. "Oh — yes — you — can!" She emphasized each word with a squeeze. "Somehow we're going to get home! You're *not* giving up now!"

Em straightened her back, set her jaw determinedly, and plodded on. Cassie's words gave her strength. Dear Cassie! How could she have survived this ordeal without her? Yes, somehow they *would* get home.

74

By the time the stars faded in the gray dawn, they had worked their way to the base of the mountain where they happened upon a small stream. There they stopped to rest. In complete exhaustion and with no thought of food to ease her hunger pangs, Em crumpled to the ground beside Cassie and instantly fell into a deep sleep.

It seemed that only minutes had passed when through dulled senses she heard the *banditos* jabbering excitedly. When she opened her eyes, she found Cassie raised on her elbows, listening intently.

"What's going on, Cassie?" she asked sleepily.

"For one thing, more *banditos* have joined us. I'm not sure what their plans are, but I heard them say something about General Ramírez y Sesma and the Mexican soldiers crossing the Rio Grande. And you won't *believe* this! They said something about Bexar! If we could just get to Bexar, we might have a chance to escape and find our way home," she whispered excitedly.

On the third day after leaving camp, they encountered and joined in the march with General Sesma and his troops. Em and Cassie were surprised to find that more than half of Sesma's army was composed of women, muledrivers, and boys. The women did all they could to help the soldiers. They carried knapsacks, prepared the food, and detoured a mile or two from the march route to find water for them. The women even attempted to build huts to protect them from inclement weather.

One evening Cassie left Em warming by the fire while she milled around the campsite. In a few minutes she came racing back looking so excited she could hardly contain herself. "Em! Listen to this news! We're headed toward Bexar, all right. I just heard some women over there say that when we reach Bexar, the Mexicans are aimin' to get even with the Texans for winning the battle there. Now, if that bit of good news won't gladden your heart, nothing will."

"Well, if that's true, it just means the Texans are

going to have to fight them again. I don't know how glad I can feel about that," said Em sadly.

"Well, I hadn't thought about it in that light," said Cassie, pausing for a moment to contemplate. Then she continued. "If you'd nose around camp with me once in a while, you'd hear lots of things. For instance, I heard that some of the soldiers disagree with their commander, General Santa Anna, about marching to Bexar. They think the army should march on Goliad instead, but they say he won't listen to reason. They say he's determined to get revenge for the insult the Mexicans suffered at Bexar, and no one can seem to change his mind about that."

Along the way, more and more convicts joined Sesma's army. They were a great asset to the army since they were well acquainted with the terrain and were skillful in waging war. But no special treatment was shown them. In fact, almost the opposite was true. Their horses were taken from them and given to the uniformed soldiers. Time and again Em and Cassie witnessed this and saw that the convicts did not even try to resist.

"What's the *matter* with them? You'd think they'd get madder than a hornet the way they're treated," said Em.

"Most of them don't mind. They say they can fight better on foot than on horseback, anyway," said Cassie.

On they marched toward Bexar. From the towns and landowners along the way, General Sesma confiscated pack mules, horses, cows, flour, corn, and other supplies the army needed. Still, the soldiers were poorly fed. Often they tramped all day without so much as a drop of water or a bite to eat. Many of the abused animals, forced to pull their heavy loads without food and water needed to sustain them, dropped dead on the way.

As they traveled across the unbroken, level plain, now and then they saw a cluster of trees or a clump of cactus dotting the nothingness and only emphasizing the emptiness of the land.

"I'm so thirsty my tongue is sticking to the roof of my mouth. I think I'll chew on a piece of cactus," said Em.

Cassie looked startled. "Em? Are you all right? You're talking crazy! Something about eating *cactus?*"

"No, I haven't lost my senses yet. Papa told me once about a man who was without water out on the desert and survived by chewing on cactus. I'm going to try it."

She snapped off several pieces and handed one to Cassie. After stripping away the hairy spines, she put a chunk of the green, fleshy fruit into her mouth and chewed until the liquid was gone. Then she spat the dry, ropey pulp to the ground.

"Not bad at all. Go ahead, Cassie. Try a piece," she urged.

Somewhat reluctantly Cassie put the piece in her mouth and began to chew slowly. A surprised look came into her eyes. "You're right. It's not bad at all. I've tasted lots worse things."

"We may go hungry, but at least we won't die of thirst as long as we can find cactus," said Em.

Suddenly the sun disappeared and the wind grew stronger. Em's skirts whipped and slapped against her legs. In a few short moments, they were enveloped in dusky darkness.

"Looks like it's going to rain buckets," said Cassie, pointing to the deep, dark cloud up above them.

"O-o-o-o!" cried Em, flinching when sharp, jagged streaks of lightning sizzled across the sky.

After a loud clap of thunder, the cloud charged with hail and lightning descended on them in all its fury. Em and Cassie ran to take refuge beneath a wispy little mesquite that offered about as much protection as holding a net over their heads. The pea-sized hail lasted only a minute, but the rain poured down in torrents.

"Look, Cassie! Here comes a soldier toward us. Wonder what he's going to do? Oh, Cassie!" Em was rigid with fear.

"Well, I'll tell you one thing. If he's got it in mind to

make us move from under this tree, he's in for a hard time," said Cassie with determination.

Much to their astonishment, he looked down at them with warm, gentle brown eyes, removed his coat, and laid it gently across their shoulders. Em raised her eyebrows in silent question as he turned and strode away.

"Can you beat that!" cried Cassie. "I didn't know there was a single person in this whole army who cared whether we lived or died."

"Maybe he has children at home that he loves very much and we remind him of them," rationalized Em. "Whatever made him do it doesn't matter. He's a kind Mexican soldier, and I'm very grateful to him."

When the rain finally slackened, they trudged on through the mire until darkness overtook them. The army encamped on a small creek and set to work cleaning their weapons and drying their soggy clothes around the small campfires.

The kind soldier who had befriended them came to reclaim his rain-soaked garment. He squatted down by their small fire and chatted for a while. His name, they learned, was Lieutenant Morales. He had left behind a family in Mexico whom he missed very much.

"What circumstances brought you to marching with our army?" he asked. He listened as Em and Cassie eagerly gave him the details of their capture by the *banditos*.

"I suspected as much," he said, staring into the depths of the glowing coals. "You have had a very difficult time, as well as your families. Don't worry, little *amigas*. I will see that not one hair on your heads is harmed while you are with me."

"We are very thankful to have you as our friend," said Em.

"Can you tell us what place this is?" asked Cassie.

"Frio River," he replied. "Not too distant from Bexar." Em and Cassie exchanged glances that showed their jubilation. Fortunately, Lieutenant Morales did not seem to notice. Their secret was safe.

The Frio River did not betray its name. The wind began to shift, and a blustery blue norther blew in that night. Snow, driven by the strong blasts, began to swirl about them. Em and Cassie were grateful when Lieutenant Morales brought them an extra blanket. Later, the thought came to Em that it might have been his own.

The next day, and the next, they trudged over the crusty snow. Shortly before they moved into Bexar, the troops were ordered to change into their dress uniforms. Exhausted from the long march, they entered Bexar late in the cold afternoon to join Santa Anna and his men and set up camp within sight of the Alamo.

13

The Siege

Bexar! So close to Mama and Papa and yet so far! Em and Cassie had not an inkling of which way to go if they dared to attempt escape. They knew that as long as they remained with the army, they would have food to eat, however scant it might be. Perhaps when they marched away from Bexar, the direction would be toward familiar territory.

Lieutenant Morales grew very impatient with his commander, General Santa Anna, soon after their arrival at Bexar. "Our spies have informed him that no more than ten occupants are within the walls of the Alamo at this very moment. Why does he wait? It would be very simple if we should attack now."

But it was not to be. The days passed and the Mexican soldiers stood ready, awaiting orders. One night as Em and Cassie huddled together on the cold, hard ground, Em could hardly believe her eyes. In the dimness she saw a single line of at least fifty or sixty dark figures slipping stealthily past the camp.

"Look, Cassie," she whispered excitedly.

"Those Mexican guards must be asleep to let this

happen," said Cassie, snickering under her breath. "Can you believe it?"

They watched as the men waded waist-deep across the narrow San Antonio River and headed for the Alamo.

"I'd swear one of them is Uncle Wash!" cried Em, moving to get up. "Let's follow them!"

Cassie grabbed her arm and pulled her back. "Lie down, Em!" she whispered. "We can't do that! One of the Mexican guards might see us and we'd give those men away. They might all be killed!"

Em lay in brooding silence for a moment. "You're right," she whispered dejectedly. "But it tears my heart out to watch him disappear from sight and not let him know we're here. Oh, Cassie! Will we ever get home?"

"You bet we will! We'll find our chance sooner or later," she encouraged.

After a long miserable period of tossing and turning, they finally dozed off.

Twelve days had passed since the Mexican army drew up before the Alamo. Cassie and Em had listened closely to the talk around the camp. The Mexicans now knew that reinforcements had entered the Alamo. They prepared themselves to do battle with any new arrivals who might try to slip in. After numerous messengers had been sent in with requests for surrender, Santa Anna became infuriated when the Texans behind the walls of the old mission refused each request. The general ranted and raved.

Lieutenant Morales, in a voice tight with anger, showed utter contempt for his leader. "Santa Anna says we must attack in order to make the enemy feel the vigor of our souls and the strength of our arms," he sneered. "Only a handful of men behind those walls against an army of *thousands*! I ask you — does that make sense? While we are showing our strength to this handful of men, General Sam Houston is assembling his army. We have tried in vain to convince our illustrious leader of

81

this, but he is too proud to listen to the recommendations of others. The time may come that he will feel much regret for what he is doing."

The ill-fated day finally arrived. Before dawn, Em and Cassie were awakened by the stirrings of the Mexican army. They crossed the river and advanced toward the Alamo.

Just as the first traces of dawn appeared, Em and Cassie heard the horrifying bugle call of death. Then the whole world erupted into deadly sounds. The mighty blasts of cannon shook the earth beneath them, and their ears rang with the sharp reports of musketry fire. In a short time, a steady stream of wounded soldiers were brought back to camp where their wounds were treated with what little medical supplies were available. The appalling sight brought the girls to the edge of hysteria.

"Cassie, what if Uncle Wash *was* with the men that slipped into the Alamo?" asked Em, blinking back tears that threatened to spill down her cheeks.

"Try not to think about it," Cassie said.

All around them lay the injured and dying Mexican soldiers. Suddenly Em grabbed Cassie's arm.

"Look!" she cried. "There's Lieutenant Morales!"

He lay as still as death on the ground among the wounded. Blood trickled from his hand. They rushed to him and Em dropped to her knees beside him.

"Lieutenant Morales!" she called. He opened pain-filled eyes.

"My little *amigas*." He smiled through his agony. "Do not worry. My hand was shattered by a bullet. Though it is very painful, it is not fatal." He grimaced then and turned his eyes toward the old fort. "The fighting has almost ended. A cease-fire has been ordered. It is not possible that a single man inside those walls is still alive. Their valiant commander fought like a true soldier to the end. A great tall man wearing a coonskin cap was captured along with six other men. General Castrillon tried to save him, but Santa Anna ordered his execution.

Some of our soldiers, trying to impress the general, fell on him with their bayonets. It was truly a horrible sight to witness." He sighed deeply and closed his eyes as though to shut out the memory.

The guns were stilled. Within the hour the main force of Mexican soldiers withdrew across the river. Rumors of the number slain or wounded spread throughout the camp. Em and Cassie listened with heavy hearts.

"Lieutenant Morales, can it be true what they say?" asked Em with tears coursing down her cheeks.

"What have you heard, my child?" he asked.

"That six hundred Texans were killed inside the Alamo and that only seventy Mexican soldiers lost their lives."

"Our general would like very much for the Mexican government to believe that so he will not look so bad. He risked the lives of such a great number of our soldiers to win this small victory," he replied.

"Look!" exclaimed Em, pointing to the woman and child being escorted from the old mission by Mexican soldiers. "Everyone did not die! Maybe Uncle Wash is still alive if he was in there!" Her hopes were instantly rekindled in her agonizing need to believe. But deep in her heart, she realized that she grasped at a straw.

14

Familiar Territory

Victory! The Alamo! Goliad! Nothing could stop them now. The Mexicans became drunk with their own power.

The Mexican army marched away from Bexar, spurred on by their colorful leader, on their way to seek out the Texas army led by Sam Houston. They no longer thought about defending their possessions. Their wish was to trample, triumph, and return home victorious. Their intense admiration and respect for Santa Anna motivated them to carry out his commands to the letter.

Not knowing what else to do, Em and Cassie plodded along behind the army in hopes that somewhere along the way they might reach a familiar area. Ahead of the army and its followers rode the little general, sitting straight and proud in his silver-trimmed saddle on the sleek, white stallion.

"Just *look* at him," sneered Cassie. "If I had my slingshot, I'd knock some of the shine off those knee-high boots. Come on, you little so-called Napoleon of the West. Take us to where we want to go."

"But what if he doesn't?" asked Em worriedly.

"Somehow we've got to find out where this army is headed," she replied.

"Maybe Lieutenant Morales can tell us," suggested Em.

"Good idea. It won't hurt to ask. Let's go find him," replied Cassie.

"That's not going to be so easy," warned Em.

Cassie was already standing on tiptoe, her eyes roving over the sea of uniformed soldiers ahead of them. With a heavy sigh, she plopped back on her heels in sheer frustration. "You're as right as rain about that, Em. There's not a button's difference in their uniforms. Oh, well! I guess we can forget that."

"Maybe not! Look!" cried Em, pointing to a soldier who dropped out of line a few paces ahead of them. He staggered over to an old elm, eased slowly to the ground, and leaned his back against the trunk.

"Is it . . . ?" Cassie strained to see. "Yes, it *is* the lieutenant!"

"Lieutenant Morales!" Em called, rushing to him.

He looked up at them with fever-bright eyes. *"Mis amigas,"* he said in a voice scarcely above a whisper.

"What's wrong, Lieutenant Morales? Are you ill?" asked Em.

"My hand pains me very much, and I am weakened from loss of blood. I must rest for a short while and then I will move on. It does not help that we have not had a morsel of food to eat all day. I wonder how much longer the men can go on under such conditions. The general is hoping to replenish supplies in Gonzales, but I do not know when we will reach there," he said.

Gonzales! Em fought to contain her joy. Cassie, however, gave an excited gasp and then quickly tried to cover it by clearing her throat. Lieutenant Morales did not seem to notice.

Suddenly a horrifying thought struck Em like a bolt of lightning. The army was advancing toward her home! Of course, that was precisely what she and Cassie had hoped for with no thought entering their minds of what could happen to their families. Perhaps the army would march away from Gonzales in another direction and would never traverse their beloved bottomlands! She decided to keep this concern to herself and not erase the joyous anticipation in Cassie's eyes.

They remained close by the side of Lieutenant Morales as the army moved toward Gonzales. More and more frequently, he was forced to stop and rest. The grueling march and lack of medical attention was taking its toll on the injured soldier. His hand was swollen to twice its size, and angry red streaks were already moving up his arm. It took all the effort he could muster to put one foot in front of the other.

Along the way they passed abandoned homes where the soldiers found pieces of furniture, spinning wheels for weaving, coffee grinders, and barns full of cotton, much of it already ginned and corded. Many pigs and chickens roamed the woods, and the soldiers went after them greedily. They stared in amazement at constructed corrals for livestock and fences around fields. Such structures were not seen in the interior of Mexico.

Finally, they moved into and across a large area of gently rolling prairie sprinkled with groves of liveoak, post oak, mesquite, elm, ash, and black walnut trees.

Em saw it first. She pulled Cassie back a few paces behind the lieutenant and pointed to their left.

"Am I dreaming or is that the river I think it is?" she whispered excitedly.

"That's it! That's it, Em!" cried Cassie, trying to keep her voice to a whisper. "The Guadalupe River we've waited so long to see." She gave Em's arm a jubilant squeeze.

The army moved along the edge of the beautiful, winding river through woods and across green valleys until they reached a point for crossing to the south side. Barges built and used by the settlers were found along the river banks.

It took several hours to move the army and all its gear to the other side. Once across, they lumbered along the bank of the river through a skirt of verdant green forest.

As they marched along the river's edge, Em's heart leaped crazily when she saw a row of giant cypress standing with their mighty roots submerged. Home could not be too far away. The landscape here was almost identical to that along the river banks behind the cabin.

As she looked here and there, feasting her eyes upon the scenery, she spied flames leaping high above the treetops ahead of them. She grabbed Cassie's arm. "Wonder what's happening? It looks like the whole world is on fire!"

In only a few moments they were able to see when they moved out of the skirt of forest. The girls stood in stunned disbelief as they watched the roof of Mr. Cole's general store collapse in a shower of sparks and a blazing roar. They were horrified when they realized that the whole town — every business establishment and dwelling — was enveloped in flames.

Lieutenant Morales sat down weakly. "So our fine general has been outsmarted. General Houston and his men have made sure that he will find no supplies for his army here. Now I wonder what great plan our leader has for us."

The irate Santa Anna moved his army along the river, taking what food that could be found in and around abandoned homes and then burning the dwellings to the ground. Em's heart sank when she came to the stark realization that the army was indeed moving toward her home on the Guadalupe! And there was the Waggoner place, the Kincaid place, the Johnsons . . . From the worried frown on Cassie's face, Em knew she harbored the same tormenting thoughts.

"We can't go much farther before they'll have to stop and make camp. It's getting late. I wonder whose place it will be," Cassie whispered fretfully. Em was too choked with anxiety to even reply.

The sun sank lower and lower on the horizon. Just ahead was the cutoff to the Waggoner place. Cassie grabbed Em's hand and squeezed it nervously. When the great white steed bearing the little general did not veer but continued to move straight ahead, Cassie breathed a shuddery sigh. Em saw her shoulders drop with relieved tension.

"It's the Kincaid place! That's where they'll *have* to make camp!" Em whispered. "It's already too late for them to go farther."

The sun had already disappeared and night was fast closing in when they moved around the bend in the trail. Em's heart leaped when she looked up ahead and saw the familiar log cabin nestled under the huge old liveoak. What a beautiful sight! Then panic gripped her. Were the Kincaids there? With all the restraint she could rally, she kept herself from running ahead to warn them. Cassie must have read her mind. Her flaming red curls bounced and swished as she shook her head vigorously and gave Em a warning frown.

Em's heart jumped wildly in her chest when the long line of soldiers and artillery rumbled up to the cabin. Santa Anna snapped his orders. A quick search was made of the cabin and the immediate surroundings. Em and Cassie waited with bated breath. Momentarily the search detail returned and stood before the little general with their report. They had found no one around the place!

Santa Anna slid from his silver-trimmed saddle, slapped the dust from his uniform, and disappeared into the cabin for the night with his aides in tow. Soon small blazing campfires dotted the area. Women and boys scurried about preparing food and making beds for the soldiers.

Thus preoccupied with their chores, they did not notice when the girls slipped away. They crawled on their hands and knees through the tall, thick grass until they reached the protective grove of trees along the river.

There they jumped to their feet and sped away through the woods as fast as they could go.

When they stopped to fill their aching lungs with air, Em said, "Cassie, I'm worried about Lieutenant Morales. I wonder what will happen to him without us. He is very sick. I wish we could have helped him more."

"I do too, but there's nothing we can do about it. Let's try not to think about him any more than we can help and put our minds on getting through these dark woods. Ready to start out again?" Em nodded. "Then let's go!"

15

The Old Comanche

To reach the cutoff to the Waggoner place, Em and Cassie doubled back over the trail the army had taken. Silvery moonlight sifted through the trees as they flew on and on through the shadowy woods. Em glanced over her shoulder from time to time, fearing they might be followed. Every bush, every stump that loomed near the trail seemed an enemy and made her heart leap into her throat.

The moment Em felt her legs would not carry her another step, Cassie pulled her from the trail into the dark shadow of a tree. What was it? Why did they stop? She did not have an ounce of breath left to ask. Neither of them could speak for a moment but could only cling to the trunk of the tree and pull great gulps of air into their lungs.

"There's a shortcut we can take and get there faster," Cassie finally said in short catches of breath. "I've never tried it in the dark, but I think I can find the way."

"N-no," gasped Em. "Let's don't try it. We might get lost, and we've been lost long enough already to last us a lifetime."

"Well, when we get back on the trail, quit looking back so much or you're going to run into a tree and kill yourself. Nobody is following us, silly. We would already know it if they were. Besides, I'm so happy to be almost home, I feel like I could skin a wildcat if it dared to get in my way."

"I'll try, but I've got the same horrible feeling I get sometimes in nightmares when I'm dreaming that a monster is following me. Like I'm trying to run but my feet are heavy as lead and won't move. It's hard not to look back."

They started out again, but this time Cassie held to a more comfortable pace. The only sound was the swish and slide of their rapidly falling footsteps on the dry grass. Suddenly from out of the dark woods came the soft, gentle call of a whippoorwill. Em caught a sharp, quick breath.

"Silly, what's the matter with you? It's just a little old bird. Don't be such a fraidy-cat. I *told* you — " Cassie's words died in her throat. Both girls stood transfixed as though turned to stone.

In the center of the moonlit trail, no more than twenty paces ahead of them, stood a Comanche. They had no warning, not even the snap of a twig nor the rustle of a leaf. For an instant they could only stand there in a misery of fear. Then somehow life returned to their limbs, and they backed away a few steps, wheeled around, and took to their heels.

"No! Come!" he called.

The pleading urgency in his voice caused them to slow their steps and look back. In the silent trail he waited, not offering to move toward them. With a wave of his arm, he motioned for them to follow. Turning and without another word, he moved noiselessly ahead of them. With muscles tense, they kept their distance several paces behind him, never relaxing a fraction of their readiness for a fast getaway.

After a time Cassie whispered, "It looks like he

*No more than twenty paces ahead of them stood
a Comanche.*

doesn't mean to harm us. And he's leading us straight toward my house. Why would he be trying to help us? This is certainly a puzzle. The only friendly Indian I ever heard of is that old Comanche outcast Matt and Memo talk with sometimes when they're in Gonzales."

"The old Comanche? Do you really think so?" asked Em, taking an intense interest in the old Indian. His dark, leathery face was covered with a mask of wrinkles. Down his back hung two silvery braids. Though he looked as old as the ages, he carried himself tall and proud like a man much younger than his years. His steps were light and quick. The fringed buckskins he wore reminded Em of Uncle Wash. He wore some much like that the day they arrived at the cabin.

They followed steadily behind the Indian until they were almost within sight of the cabin. Then Cassie took Em's hand and pulled her along at a run.

"Come on! We're home! We're home!" she cried. They whisked past the old Indian, raced across the front yard, and bounded up the porch steps.

"Mama! Mama! It's Cassie. We're home!"

Cassie pushed on the heavy door. It creaked open. How positively strange! Her mother was always very careful to bar the doors at night. They eased cautiously into the dark room. In the eerie stillness, Em could hear the thump-thump-thump of her heart in her chest.

"Mama? Mama?" Cassie called into the blackness. They waited for some sound, some response. Only dead stillness reigned. She sighed and groped for Em's hand, and they backed slowly onto the porch. There in the cold, moonwashed night stood the old Comanche waiting silently.

"They're gone. But where?" Cassie's trembling voice was heavy with disappointment.

To Em it seemed as if this were all happening in a bad dream. They were home, but not one familiar face had they seen.

"The folks along the river must have been warned

93

that the Mexican army is headed this way. I wonder if Mama and Papa have left too," pondered Em. "I can't help how tired we are, Cassie. We've got to get over there and find out."

"Come," said the old Comanche.

This time they followed him gratefully. He headed straight through the woods toward Em's home.

"Wonder how he knows where we live?"

"He's probably wandered around in these woods for so long he knows exactly where every family lives along this river," said Cassie.

As they worked their way through the woods, thoughts and questions whirled in Em's mind. Would she find Mama and Papa at home? She had mixed feelings about that. In one tiny corner of her heart she hoped to find them there, but her common sense told her it would be better if they had fled since the Mexican army was so near.

But what if they *were* gone? What would she and Cassie do? Where would they go? She shook her head. She would think about that later. Had Papa recovered from his injury? If not, was this the aged Indian outcast who might help him? He must be! He had taken it upon himself to help her and Cassie find their way through the dark woods, hadn't he? Matt had told her about the old Indian who had lost favor with other members of his tribe because he was too friendly and helpful to the settlers. He had shown them ways to survive in the wilderness and how to make clothing out of buckskin.

Though they had traveled from early morning light to deep night, her steps grew stronger and more determined as they neared the cabin. Every tree, every leaf seemed to whisper welcome to her. She thought her heart would burst when her eyes finally came to rest on the cabin nestled in the shadows.

"Oh, Cassie! Reckon they're home?" asked Em anxiously.

"We certainly won't find out standing here. Come on," said Cassie.

They raced toward the cabin. As they crossed the yard, Em began to call.

"Mama! Papa!" she cried. They dashed up the steps and pushed on the front door, but it did not budge. They waited with bated breath.

The awful clamp around Em's heart eased its icy grip when she heard the slide of the bar. The door swung open and there stood Mama. She uttered not a sound but gathered both girls hungrily into her arms and held them as though she would never let go.

Then she took a deep, sobbing breath. "Oh, Em! Cassie! You're back! You've come back!" She rocked them gently back and forth, murmuring their names as if she could not get enough assurance that they were really there. Then she held them at arm's length, feasting her eyes upon them. "What happened? Who took you? Where have you been? We had lost all hope of ever seeing you again."

"We never thought we'd ever get home either, Mama. The *banditos* took us far away from here. It was awful," said Em, tightening her arms around Mama's waist. Then she looked up at her mother and asked, "Where's Papa?"

"He didn't even stir when I got up to come to the door. Sometimes he sleeps so soundly, it scares me. He doesn't even know you're here. Come. Let's go wake him. He'll be so happy. After you were taken away, he seemed to give up trying to get better. This has all been so hard for him."

"Why didn't you leave, Mama? Didn't you get word that the Mexican army was headed this way? They're camped at the Kincaid place this very night. We've got to leave here right away. The army will be on the move at dawn, and that's only a few hours from now."

"Yes, we got word. Martha and the children didn't

want to leave without us, but I was afraid your papa couldn't stand the trip."

"We've *got* to go, Mama, and we don't have a minute to spare! We can't stay here!"

"But, honey — "

"No, Mama. We've *got* to go. Santa Anna is very angry because the Texans burned Gonzales and all the supplies he had hoped to get there for his army. Now they're burning every home they pass. We can't risk staying here."

"She's right, Aunt Miriam. It would be too dangerous to stay," said Cassie. "He's threatened to drive every American out of Texas, to shoot everyone found with guns in their hands, and to destroy all property. He says that when he has made his coffee with water from the Sabine River, he'll return victorious to Mexico City."

"But, Em, your papa! I don't know . . . ," fretted Mama.

Em went into the room where Papa slept. She looked down at his pale face then leaned over and kissed his cheek. He did not stir but continued to sleep soundly. Poor Papa! But she felt sure his condition would change for the better soon. She would talk to the old Comanche about it the very first chance she had once they got on the trail. At the moment, though, there was no time. They had to move fast.

Mama issued instructions to the girls. They scurried about the cabin helping her get together bedding, clothes, and food supplies.

"There's no way to know whether or not we have plenty," said Mama, surveying the provisions they had amassed. "Now I've got to go harness Old Jake and Hannah to the wagon. They're in the lot. It's a good thing I didn't put them out to pasture last night." She opened the door and started to step outside but immediately slammed it closed again and slid the bar across.

"What is it?" cried the frightened girls in chorus.

"An old Indian is out there with Jake and Hannah already hitched to the wagon!"

Em heaved a relieved sigh. "It's all right, Mama. He's our friend. He led us through the woods." She opened the door and motioned to him.

In the late, late night he helped them load the supplies. Then he lifted Papa from the bed, carried him out to the wagon, and laid him on the soft bed of quilts. Em, Cassie, and Mama climbed onto the wagon seat. The old Comanche handed Mama the reins then slapped Old Jake's rump to get him started. When the wagon began to roll, he walked beside it for a while then vanished into the night before they even realized he was gone.

16

The Runaways

The wagon rumbled through the night along the dark, lonely trail. Deserted farm houses they passed stood eerily silent, but Mama never failed to call out as they approached. Then she would crack the reins to coax Old Jake and Hannah to move faster. But true to his nature, Old Jake seemed to know precisely what to do to provoke anger in even the mildest-tempered human being. No matter how often Mama cracked the reins, he refused to be driven at a pace beyond a crawl.

"Let me at him!" Cassie finally shouted in exasperation. Before Mama could issue a word of warning, she jumped to the tongue of the wagon and promptly leaped upon Old Jake's back. "Giddy-up, you stubborn old mule! Yeeeow! Come on! Those Mexicans will make stew meat out of you if you don't get a move on!"

She flopped and bounced around on his back, but he would not be intimidated. Instead, he surprised her with some tricks of his own. The thick hide on his back began to roll from side to side. She swayed to the right and then to the left, holding onto the harness with all her might to keep from toppling to the ground. She braced for another roll, but he surprised her again by stiffening his front legs and bouncing her a foot into the air with each step he took. Her red hair flapped and swished into a tangled muss.

"You just go ahead, Jake. Try all your tricks, but you won't get rid of me! I'll show you I can be as stubborn as you are!" shouted Cassie.

"Hang on!" cried Em. Mama watched in dismay.

"After this crazy ride, I think I'm ready to start breaking mustangs. It couldn't be much harder than trying to stay on Old Jake," she replied breathlessly.

Cassie persevered until Jake finally decided to settle down and work in harmony with Hannah, moving the wagon along at a decent pace. Then Cassie climbed back onto the wagon seat.

The wagon rumbled along the dark trail. Papa seemed to be resting comfortably on his thick bed of quilts. Em and Cassie began telling Mama about their capture by the *banditos,* their ordeal in the mountains of Coahuila, and how they finally reached home by following the Mexican army. Em could not bring herself to tell Mama about the Alamo and her fears for Uncle Wash.

They had scarcely finished their story when they suddenly came upon a log cabin. Mama called out as she always did. To their surprise, a sleepy-faced young woman stepped onto the moonlit porch.

"The Mexicans are coming! You must get ready to leave now!" called Mama. "The Mexican army is camped a few miles back and will be marching this way early in the morning."

Four small children rushed onto the porch and clung to the woman. She looked down at them fretfully and then back at Mama. "The Mexicans! Oh, what will I do? George, my husband, left to join up with Houston's army. I don't know if I can handle this all by myself. Grandpa is old and almost like a child himself, and I have these four little ones," she said helplessly.

"You must come with us. We'll help you," coaxed Mama. "But we've got to hurry!"

The woman rushed over to the bed in the dog-trot. "Grandpa! The Mexicans are comin'! Get up! We've got to go!"

"Eh?" he said, cupping a hand to his ear.

"Get up! The Mexicans are comin'! We've got to go!" she repeated loudly.

"It's about to *snow*?"

"No, Grandpa! We've got to go! The Mexicans are comin'!" she yelled in his ear.

Without a word he sprang up, slapped his hat on his grizzled head, and snatched his gun from under the bed. Then on his bowed legs and in his long underwear, he hurried into the yard.

"Where are they? By gum! Just let me at 'em!" he roared, looking here and there with his gun poised.

The young woman flew across the yard to him, shouting as she went. "Grandpa! Get your clothes on and go hitch the oxen to the cart. We've got to leave here as fast as we can!"

"Oh!" he said, looking embarrassed and hurrying back into the dog-trot to pull on his clothes.

Em and Cassie quieted the frightened, whimpering children while Mama and the woman set to work gathering up supplies. The old man struck out toward the barn and returned in a few minutes with the oxen and cart.

The woman flung items into the cart, piling them in a helter-skelter heap. Em and Cassie set the children on top of the pile and in short order they were moving along the trail. The frantic young mother drove the oxen mercilessly while the old man stumbled along behind the cart.

"If that thing holds together until we get out of sight of the house, it'll be a miracle," said Cassie, pointing to the cart's wobbling wooden wheels.

When the early morning sun began to edge its way above the horizon, they joined a long line of men, women, and children. The people were walking, riding on horse-back, in carts, on sleds, and in wagons — hurrying as fast as they could go in their flight from the Mexicans. Occasionally a rider galloped by shouting warnings that the enemy was rapidly approaching. Filled with panic, many of the colonists threw bedding, clothes, and other provisions out of their wagons and carts to lighten the loads in order to move faster. Only when they were unable to travel any farther in a day would the runaways stop and make camp for the night.

Each time they stopped, they found that their group had increased in number. No greater show of humanity was ever displayed. All were friends, countrymen who had a feeling of wondrous kindness toward one another. No morsel of food was withheld from the hungry. When someone suffered an illness, many gentle hands reached out to give tender care.

One late evening while Mama and Papa sat around their small campfire chatting with the young woman and the old man, Cassie began to twitch restlessly. Finally she bounded to her feet and said, "Come on, Em. Let's stroll around the camp and see if we can find anyone we know."

"Which way should we go? This camp stretches for miles and miles. I can't see the end of the line behind us or ahead of us," said Em.

"Let's walk up ahead this time," said Cassie.

They occasionally stopped to chat as they meandered through the camp. But Cassie's restless nature kept them on the move, always searching for a familiar face. Em was beginning to wonder if Cassie ever intended to turn around and go back to their wagon. She was about to mention it when at a distance they saw a small child toddling toward them.

"Poor little thing! She must be lost. We'll have to find her family," said Em.

They rushed toward her. Suddenly, Cassie clapped her hand to her heart.

"Rachel!" she squealed. Her baby sister ran into her arms. She picked her up and smothered her with hugs and kisses.

"They're here! Right here in this camp!" cried Em excitedly.

"Rachel, where's Mama?" asked Cassie.

The baby smiled, wrapped her chubby arms around her neck, and planted a wet kiss on her cheek. "Wachel pway," she said in her baby language.

"I forgot she can't talk enough to tell us anything. I'm not even sure she remembers me," said Cassie disappointedly.

"We'll find them. We'll walk this camp over until we do," said Em with resolve. "She's wandered away from them, and they're probably looking everywhere for her right now."

"Rachel! Rachel!" came a voice from behind them. Turning, they saw Joe racing toward them with a distraught look on his face.

"Joe!" cried Cassie.

"Cassie? Is that you, Cassie? Em?" he asked uncertainly, looking as if he had seen two ghosts.

"Yes, Joe," said Cassie, standing Rachel on the ground beside her and reaching to hug him. "Where's Mama?"

"We're camped up ahead a ways," he said. "Mama will be so happy. What happened? Where have you been? We thought you'd never come back. We've all been so worried."

"We'll tell you all about it. Take us to Mama first."

They saw Aunt Martha before she saw them. With the other children in tow, she was darting from one camp to another calling for Rachel. When she finally saw them, the color drained from her face and she began to sputter, "C-C-Cassie? Em?" Then her legs folded and she crumpled to the ground.

It took a while to revive Aunt Martha to the point that she could even talk. She would hug them and then stare at them, unbelieving. Then she would hug them again, half sobbing and half laughing. When she finally got herself together and when she felt that her legs were strong enough to carry her, Em and Cassie led her and the children to their camp. Aunt Martha wanted to hear every detail about their ordeal.

"We fear the Mexicans and are running from them, but we have one of them to thank for being kind to Em and Cassie," Mama told Aunt Martha.

"Lieutenant Morales was so good to us," said Em. "I wonder if his hand is better and if he is getting well. He was awfully sick when we left him."

"Well, we can certainly hope and pray that the good man is much better," said Aunt Martha. Little Rachel yawned and laid her head in Cassie's lap.

"I wonder how many days we've traveled so close together and didn't realize it," said Cassie.

"It's so good to know we're all together again," said Mama.

"Yes," said Em as she snuggled closer to her.

17

Home Again!

About mid-morning Em heard a muffled noise coming from behind the long winding line of runaways. The noise grew more and more distinct. She looked back and saw a rider speeding toward them, waving his arms and shouting. As he passed along the weary line of people, they suddenly began to shout and leap around, throwing hats and bonnets into the air.

As he sped past the wagon, he shouted to Mama, "Turn around and go home! The Texas army has beaten the Mexicans! Go home! It's over!" He heralded the news up and down the line.

"Zeb! Em! Did you hear that? We can go home!" Mama was so happy, she hugged them both, crying tears of joy. "We can go home, Zeb, where Em and I can give you proper care. Everything is going to be fine now. I just know it will. We have Em back and we're going home! That ought to make you feel better already."

Papa smiled. His eyes brightened, but Em could tell that the trip had taken its toll on him.

The journey back was long and hard, but after several days they reached familiar territory and excitement mounted. What would they find when they finally reached home? Would Uncle Wash be there? What about Matt, Memo, Uncle Karl, Mr. Kincaid, and Uncle Anson? What had happened to Matt's mother, Little Bruce, and Aunt Molly? Where were they? Numerous questions raced through Em's mind as she jiggled on the wagon seat beside Mama.

They passed charred fields and piles of rubble where settlers' homes once stood. Was this what they could expect to find when they reached their home on the Guadalupe?

"It won't be long until we reach the Kincaid place," said Mama, breathing a weary sigh.

"I almost dread it after what we've seen. I don't think there's much hope that their home is still standing since the Mexican army camped there," fretted Em.

A moment before the wagon rolled into sight of the cabin, Em squeezed her eyes tightly shut. Fear gripped her until she could hardly breathe. When she heard Mama gasp, she felt like she would faint.

"Open your eyes, honey! Look! Oh, Zeb! They didn't get burned out! Maybe there's hope for our place too!"

Em could hardly believe her eyes. Not only was the cabin still standing, but there stood Mrs. Kincaid in the yard waving to them. Aunt Molly stood beside her holding Little Bruce.

When the wagons creaked to a standstill, the children jumped to the ground squealing joyfully. Little Bruce squirmed out of Aunt Molly's arms to join in the frolic, laughing and squealing as if it were the thing to do because everyone else was doing it. That made the children laugh harder.

"There are so many questions — I don't know what to ask first," said Mrs. Kincaid, offering her hand to help Mama step to the ground.

Before Aunt Molly could waddle over to help, Aunt Martha had already managed to get down from the wagon all by herself. "Goodness! Oh, my goodness!" Aunt

Molly exclaimed breathlessly, hugging Aunt Martha and then gathering as many of the children into her arms as she could.

"We knew that Em and Cassie had escaped from the Mexicans, but we didn't know what happened after that," said Mrs. Kincaid. Em and Cassie turned around quickly and gave her a puzzled look. "Let's get Zeb into the house. Miriam, I know you and Martha are anxious to get home to see how things are, but Molly and I are going to insist that you stay right here with us tonight. I know these children are tired and hungry, and it won't take Molly and me but a minute to whip up something for all of us to eat."

Mrs. Kincaid rushed into the cabin to prepare a place for Papa while Mama and Aunt Molly helped him up the steps. Em and Cassie followed them into the kitchen, leaving the younger children in the yard to romp and play.

When they got Papa settled comfortably, Mrs. Kincaid said, "Now, Miriam and Martha, you two sit right down over there at the table. I've got some coffee already brewed. You just sit there and drink your coffee. Molly and I will have something fixed in no time."

Em stood on one foot and then the other, waiting for a chance to break into the conversation without being rude. But the talk went on without letup.

"Yep, Santa Anna and his army never knew we were within hollerin' distance of them when we were down there on the river hiding in Matt's and Memo's cave. They left the place in pretty much of a mess, but from what you've told us about the number of places you saw that were burned, we are very thankful to have a roof over our heads. I couldn't believe they didn't even go near our place," said Aunt Molly, shaking her head in wonder as she bustled about the kitchen.

"Speaking of Matt and Memo — where are those two?" asked Mama. Well, at least Em was going to hear the answer to one of her questions.

106

A fretful look came into Mrs. Kincaid's eyes. She breathed a heavy sigh. "They followed the Mexican army. Matt left a note saying they were going to follow the Mexicans because they would lead them to Houston's army where they could get with Jonathan and Anson and help fight. When they get home, I won't know whether to hug them to death or tar and feather them."

Aunt Molly laughed. "Now, Sarah, you know exactly what you'll do. Hug them *nearly* to death, of course."

A tiny pause gave Em her chance. "Mrs. Kincaid, how did you know we escaped from the Mexicans? Did you see us?"

"Oh! How thoughtless of me! I should have known you would be wondering. One of the Mexican soldiers — a Lieutenant Morales — was very ill with a wounded hand."

"Lieutenant Morales!" Em and Cassie chorused, leaning forward with undivided attention.

"Yes, he was so ill he couldn't travel. The army left without him. That poor man was almost dead when we found him. His hand became infected and poisoned his whole body. I don't know what we would have done if that old Comanche hadn't wandered by here."

"Comanche?" asked Em with interest.

"Yes, the one Matt and Memo know. Molly and I had tried every remedy we knew to try on the Mexican soldier. The old Indian just happened to be wandering by one day, and I remembered how he was supposed to be so good at curing the sick. I got him to come into the house to look at Lieutenant Morales.

"Then he went out into the woods and was gone for about an hour before he came back and asked me for a kettle. He boiled something on a little fire he built out in the yard. Then we saw him crushing something. It looked like it might have been something like prickly pear. He acted like he much preferred to be left alone at his work, so Molly and I didn't venture near enough to see what it was. Anyway, he spooned some of the liquid down Lieu-

107

tenant Morales and put a poultice on his hand. We could see improvement the very next day. Before he was able to travel, he told us about the two Anglo girls named Em and Cassie. He was shocked but glad to learn that the army had led you home."

What wonderful news! Lieutenant Morales was alive and on his way back to his family in Mexico. Well, that settled it. Em felt sure Mama would have no objection to having the old Comanche come to work his cure on Papa. She could hardly wait for Matt and Memo to get home and find him.

18

Help for Papa

After rumbling along in the wagon for days on end, Em felt like a bird free of its cage. While the younger children raced around the yard laughing and playing with Little Bruce, she sat quietly on the porch steps beside Cassie, drinking in the beauty that surrounded her.

Everywhere signs of spring had emerged, showing the birth of a new earth. Bushes covered with tiny, tender buds basked in the early morning sun. Sprigs of grass scattered patches of green all around. Trees were already beginning to unfurl their leaves, and here and there a splash of color caught the eye where tight little clumps of delicate spring flowers had burst into full bloom. What a gloriously beautiful time of the year!

Em felt a serenity she had not experienced in a long time. Here she was, back on the Guadalupe with Mama and Papa. The war was over, and the men who had gone to fight were returning home. Matt and Memo were coming home. Even Cassie, in one of her weak moments, had let it slip that she was looking forward to the time when they were home again. Of course, she swore Em to secrecy about that little matter.

Em felt happy, but two concerns tormented her. Uncle Wash — could he have been at the Alamo? And Papa — there was a miserably slow improvement in his condition even during their runaway from the Mexicans. But that was just it. His recuperation was too prolonged to suit her. If she only knew where to find the old Comanche, she would bring him to Papa.

Her thoughts were interrupted when Mama and Aunt Martha came out of the cabin with their arms laden with quilts. They had taken them from the wagons the evening before to make pallets for sleeping. Em and Cassie jumped up to help them.

"Em, make Papa's bed in the wagon while I hitch up Old Jake and Hannah so we can start for home," said Mama.

"Cassie, help me round up the little ones and get them in the wagon. If your father happens to get home and doesn't find us, it will frighten him to death," said Aunt Martha.

After much to-do, the wagons finally moved out with many hearty waves to Mrs. Kincaid, Aunt Molly, and Little Bruce. The Waggoners rolled ahead with five happy little faces hanging out of the rear of the canvas-covered wagon. Cassie sat beside Aunt Martha on the wagon seat, occasionally looking back and calling out to tell Em just one more thing.

All of a sudden a thought out of the blue popped into Em's head. Not once in weeks had she heard Cassie mention a slingshot! She was still the same slap-dash girl who plunged headlong into anything she did. Yet, upon reflection, Em could see a subtle change. Could Cassie be growing up? She smiled thoughtfully.

When the moment came that the wagons went their separate ways, Em felt a tug of loneliness even before the Waggoners disappeared from sight. For days they had been together like one big family. She would miss that rowdy, lovable brood. On the other hand, joy filled her heart when she thought of finally being in the solitude of her own home with her cozy bed in the loft.

"Mama, look at Old Jake. He must know we're almost home. He's actually put some life into his steps," said Em.

Papa raised up from his bed to look. "Well, that old scalawag! He does have a little spirit left in him, doesn't he?"

When they rolled into the clearing, Mama gave a joyful cry. "Zeb! Em! There it is! The Mexican army must not have even passed here. Everything looks fine from here."

When the wagon creaked to a standstill in the front yard, Mama and Em hurried inside. The house had not been disturbed. Mama placed a chair on the front porch for Papa to rest in while she and Em unloaded the wagon.

After they emptied the wagon, Mama clucked at Old Jake and Hannah. "Just a few more steps and your long journey will be at an end after you pull the wagon to the barn," said Mama.

Em darted around the corner of the house and headed for the barn lot. On the way, she stopped to peek inside the smokehouse. Great slabs of cured meat still hung from pot hooks in the ceiling.

It was as though they had never been gone. However, she no longer heard the cluck of chickens and the gobble of turkeys in the barnyard. They must have taken to the woods in search of food.

When Em reached the barn, she picked up an armload of fodder and dumped it in the corner of the lot for Old Jake and Hannah. They would have a feast this time, and they deserved every crunchy bite after pulling the wagon day in and day out for numerous days. For an extra special treat, she mixed with it a few ears of dried corn.

After careful inspection of the place, Mama was very satisfied to find it in good shape. In no time at all, activity was back to normal.

It was mid-afternoon when they finally sat down on the front porch with Papa to enjoy a few quiet moments of rest. No one spoke, but words did not seem necessary. How good it was just to lean back and indulge oneself in the solitude of home!

Suddenly the quiet was broken by the rumbling of wagon wheels moving nearer. In a moment the wagons rolled into the clearing. The Waggoners! The Kincaids! The Johnsons! And there were Matt and Memo jogging along beside them on their horses. They were home! But why were they coming for a visit at such an odd time?

Em's eyes searched each wagon. There was Mr. Kincaid — and Uncle Karl — and Uncle Anson. All of the men — except Uncle Wash! Where was Uncle Wash?

When Matt slid from the saddle and walked up to the porch, Em saw that familiar old pouch in his hand that contained the prized collection of arrowheads. Then she knew. She *had* seen Uncle Wash slip into the Alamo. Somehow deep within her she had known all along.

"He wanted you to have it," said Matt simply, and he handed the pouch to her.

"But you weren't at the Alamo with him, were you?" she asked tearfully. Cassie laid an arm across her shoulders.

"No, but we heard that Mrs. Dickinson and her little girl were the only survivors. We found out where she was and on our way home we stopped to talk with her. Before the battle started, Mr. Wash gave her the pouch of arrowheads and asked if she would see that you got these if anything happened to him and she should get out alive. Mrs. Dickinson said those brave men never gave up but fought valiantly to the end. That handful of men — 180 brave Texans — killed over 1,500 Mexican soldiers within an hour," said Matt, shaking his head in wonder.

"But their General Santa Anna bragged that his soldiers killed six hundred Texans and that only seventy Mexican soldiers lost their lives," said Em.

"Yes, Em, but you remember when Lieutenant Morales acted as if he didn't believe that story either," said Cassie.

"Lieutenant Morales?" asked Memo.

"We'll tell you all about our friend sometime," said Cassie.

"I think we must all have plenty to tell each other," replied Memo.

"This news about Uncle Wash is really going to be hard on Papa, I'm afraid," said Em. "Matt, I've wished for a long time that you and Memo were here to find the old Comanche. I'd like for you to bring him here to see Papa. He's got to get well. Mama and I need him so much."

"You won't believe this, Em, but we saw him wandering through the woods when we were on our way over here. Come on, Memo!" he said, vaulting into his saddle.

Within the hour they returned. Sitting straight and proud on the horse with Matt was the Comanche who had led Em and Cassie through the dark woods. Mama smiled and was very gracious when she ushered him into the room where Papa now rested on his bed.

Em still held the pouch of arrowheads in her hand. She strolled out into the yard a ways from the house. Matt followed her while Cassie and Memo sat down on the porch steps together.

"Matt, as much as you have always admired Uncle Wash's arrowhead collection, I know he would be very pleased to know that I am sharing them with you," Em said, reaching into the pouch.

When she laid the arrowheads in his hand, his eyes grew wide. "Wow! Are you sure?"

"Yes. You will have half of the collection and I will have the other half. That's the way I want it. Each time we look at our share, it will remind us of what good friends we truly are and always will be." She reached down and plucked the little wildflower near her foot and turned it tenderly in her hand. "You see this bluebonnet?"

"Bluebonnet?" he asked with a puzzled look on his face.

"Yes. Bluebonnet." She held the little flower so Matt could have a closer look. "See? The little blue blossoms are shaped like tiny bonnets. That's the reason I call it bluebonnet. The very first flower I ever picked in Texas when we were on our way to the Guadalupe to start a new life was one just like this. It got all mangled and crushed and I almost cried. But Mama told me that every spring would bring lovely fields of them for me to pick. She was right. And just as sure as the spring will always bring the bluebonnet, that's how sure I am that Papa is going to be strong and healthy again. And we'll all enjoy many happy years on the Guadalupe near good friends and neighbors. Thank you, Matt, for bringing the old Comanche."

As they strolled back to the porch to sit with Cassie and Memo, Em said, "Won't it be fun growing up together on the Guadalupe, Matt?" He nodded, kicked a pebble with the toe of his boot, and smiled timidly at her.

Bibliography

de la Pena, José Enrique. *With Santa Anna in Texas.* College
Station: Texas A&M University Press, 1975.
Quarterly of the Texas State Historical Association, IV, 160–
169 (The Runaway Scrape).